PREFACE.

The plan of "Graded and Higher Lessons in English" will perhaps be better understood if we first speak of two classes of text-books with which this course is brought into competition.

+Method of One Class of Text-books+.—In one class are those that aim chiefly to present a course of technical grammar in the order of Orthography, Etymology, Syntax, and Prosody. These books give large space to grammatical Etymology, and demand much memorizing of definitions, rules, declensions, and conjugations, and much formal word parsing,—work of which a considerable portion is merely the invention of grammarians, and has little value in determining the pupil's use of language or in developing his reasoning faculties. This is a revival of the long-endured, unfruitful, old-time method.

+Method of Another Class of Text-books+.—In another class are those that present a miscellaneous collection of lessons in Composition, Spelling, Pronunciation, Sentence-analysis, Technical Grammar, and General Information, without unity or continuity. The pupil who completes these books will have gained something by practice and will have picked up some scraps of knowledge; but his information will be vague and disconnected, and he will have missed that mental training which it is the aim of a good text-book to afford. A text-book is of value just so far as it presents a clear, logical development of its subject. It must present its science or its art as a natural growth, otherwise there is no apology for its being.

+The Study of the Sentence for the Proper Use of Words+.—It is the plan of this course to trace with easy steps the natural development of the sentence, to consider the leading facts first and then to descend to the details. To begin with the parts of speech is to begin with details and to disregard the higher unities, without which the details are scarcely intelligible. The part of speech to which a word belongs is determined only by its function in the sentence, and inflections simply mark the offices and relations of words. Unless the pupil has been systematically trained to discover the functions and relations of words as elements of an organic whole, his knowledge of the parts of speech is of little value. It is not because he cannot conjugate the verb or decline the pronoun that he falls into such errors as "How many sounds *have* each of the vowels?" "Five years' interest *are* due." "She is older than *me*." He probably would not say "each *have*," "interest *are*," "*me* am." One thoroughly familiar with the structure of the sentence will find little trouble in using correctly the few inflectional forms in English.

+The Study of the Sentence for the Laws of Discourse+.—Through the study of the sentence we not only arrive at an intelligent knowledge of the parts of speech and a correct use of grammatical forms, but we discover the laws of discourse in general. In the sentence the student should find the law of unity, of continuity, of proportion, of order. All good writing consists of good sentences properly joined. Since the sentence is the foundation or unit of discourse, it is all-important that the pupil should know the sentence. He should be able to put the principal and the subordinate parts in their proper relation; he should know the exact function of every element, its relation to other elements and its relation to the whole. He should know the sentence as the skillful engineer knows his engine, that, when there is a disorganization of parts, he may at once find the difficulty and the remedy for it.

+The Study of the Sentence for the Sake of Translation+.—The laws of thought being the same for all nations, the logical analysis of the sentence is the same for all languages. When a student who has acquired a knowledge of the English sentence comes to the translation of a foreign language, he finds his work greatly simplified. If in a sentence of his own language he sees only a mass of unorganized words, how much greater must be his confusion when this mass of words is in a foreign tongue! A study of the parts of speech is a far less important preparation for translation, since the declensions and conjugations in English do not conform to those of other languages. Teachers of the classics and of modern languages are beginning to appreciate these facts.

+The Study of the Sentence for Discipline+.—As a means of discipline nothing can compare with a training in the logical analysis of the sentence. To study thought through its outward form, the sentence, and to discover the fitness of the different parts of the expression to the parts of the thought, is to learn to think. It has been noticed that pupils thoroughly trained in the analysis and the construction of sentences come to their other studies with a decided advantage in mental power. These results can be obtained only by systematic and persistent work. Experienced teachers understand that a few weak lessons on the sentence at the beginning of a course and a few at the end can afford little discipline and little knowledge that will endure, nor can a knowledge of the sentence be gained by memorizing complicated rules and labored forms of analysis. To compel a pupil to wade through a page or two of such bewildering terms as "complex adverbial element of the second class" and "compound prepositional adjective phrase," in order to comprehend a few simple functions, is grossly unjust; it is a substitution of form for content, of words for ideas.

+Subdivisions and Modifications after the Sentence+.—Teachers familiar with text books that group all grammatical instruction around the eight parts of speech, making eight independent units, will not, in the following lessons, find everything in its accustomed place. But, when it is remembered that the thread of connection unifying this work is the sentence, it will be seen that the lessons fall into their natural order of sequence. When, through the development of the sentence, all the offices of the different parts of speech are mastered, the most natural thing is to continue the work of classification and subdivide the parts of speech. The inflection of words, being distinct from their classification, makes a separate division of the work. If the chief end of grammar were to enable one to parse, we should not here depart from long-established precedent.

+Sentences in Groups—Paragraphs+.—In tracing the growth of the sentence from the simplest to the most complex form, each element, as it is introduced, is illustrated by a large number of detached sentences, chosen with the utmost care as to thought and expression. These compel the pupil to confine his attention to one thing till he gets it well in hand. Paragraphs from literature are then selected to be used at intervals, with questions and suggestions to enforce principles already presented, and to prepare the way informally for the regular lessons that follow. The lessons on these selections are, however, made to take a much wider scope. They lead the pupil to discover how and why sentences are grouped into paragraphs, and how paragraphs are related to each other; they also lead him on to discover whatever is most worthy of imitation in the style of the several models presented.

+The Use of the Diagram+.—In written analysis, the simple map, or diagram, found in the following lessons, will enable the pupil to present directly and vividly to the eye the exact function of every clause in the sentence, of every phrase in the clause, and of every word in the phrase—to picture the complete analysis of the sentence, with principal and subordinate parts in their proper relations. It is only by the aid of such a map, or picture, that the pupil can, at a single view, see the sentence as an organic whole made up of many parts performing various functions and standing in various relations. Without such map he must labor under the disadvantage of seeing all these things by piecemeal or in succession.

But, if for any reason the teacher prefers not to use these diagrams, they may be omitted without causing the slightest break in the work. The plan of this book is in no way dependent on the use of the diagrams.

+The Objections to the Diagram+.—The fact that the pictorial diagram groups the parts of a sentence according to their offices and relations, and not in the order of speech, has been spoken of as a fault. It is on the contrary, a merit, for it teaches the pupil to look through the literary order and discover the logical order. He thus learns what the literary order really is, and sees that this may be varied indefinitely, so long as the logical relations are kept clear.

The assertion that correct diagrams can be made mechanically is not borne out by the facts. It is easier to avoid precision in oral analysis than in written. The diagram drives the pupil to a most searching examination of the sentence, brings him face to face with every difficulty, and compels a decision on every point.

+The Abuse of the Diagram+.—Analysis by diagram often becomes so interesting and so helpful that, like other good things, it is liable to be overdone. There is danger of requiring too much written analysis. When the ordinary constructions have been made clear, diagrams should be used only for the more difficult sentences, or, if the sentences are long, only for the more difficult parts of them. In both oral and written analysis there is danger of repeating what needs no repetition. When the diagram has served its purpose, it should be dropped.

SUGGESTIONS FOR COMPOSITION EXERCISES

The exercises in composition found in the numbered Lessons of this book are generally confined to the illustration and the practical application of the principles of the science as these principles are developed step by step. To break up the continuity of the text by thrusting unrelated composition work between lessons closely related and mutually dependent is exceedingly unwise.

The Composition Exercises suggested in this revision of "Graded Lessons" are designed to review the regular Lessons and to prepare in a broad, informal way for text work that follows. But since these Exercises go much farther, and teach the pupil how to construct paragraphs and how to observe and imitate what is good in different authors, they are placed in a supplement, and not between consecutive Lessons of the text.

To let such general composition work take the place of the regular grammar lesson, say once a week, will be profitable. We suggest that the sentence work on the selections in the Supplement be made to follow Lessons 30, 40, 50, 60, 70, 77; but each teacher must determine for himself when these and the other outlined lessons can best be used. We advise that other selections from literature be made and these exercises continued with the treatment of the parts of speech.

For composition work to precede Lesson 30 we suggest that the teacher break up a short story of one or two paragraphs into simple sentences, making some of these transposed, some interrogative, and some exclamatory. The pupils may be required to copy these, to underline the subject and the predicate, and to tell, in answer to suggestive questions, what some of the other words and groups of words do (the questions on the selections in the Supplement may aid the teacher). The pupils may then write out the story in full form. To vary the exercise, the teacher might read the story and let the pupils write out the short sentences.

A TALK ON LANGUAGE.

The teacher is recommended, before assigning any lesson, to occupy the time of at least two or three recitations, in talking with his pupils about language, always remembering that, in order to secure the interest of his class, he must allow his pupils to take an active part in the exercise. The teacher should guide the thought of his class; but, if he attempt to do *all the talking*, he will find, when he concludes, that he has been left to do *all the thinking*.

We give below a few hints in conducting this talk on language, but the teacher is not expected to confine himself to them. He will, of course, be compelled, in some instances, to resort to various devices in order to obtain from the pupils answers equivalent to those here suggested.

+Teacher+.—I will pronounce these three sounds very slowly and distinctly, thus: *b-u-d*. Notice, it is the *power*, or *sound*, of the letter, and not its name, that I give. What did you hear?

+Pupil+.—I heard three sounds.

+T.—+Give them. I will write on the board, so that you can see them, three letters—*b-u-d*. Are these letters, taken separately, signs to you of anything?

+P.—+Yes, they are signs to me of the three sounds that I have just heard.

+T.—+What then do these letters, taken separately, picture to your eye?

+P.—+They picture the sounds that came to my ear.

+T+.—Letters then are the signs of what?

+P.—Letters are the signs of sounds+.

+T+.—I will pronounce the same three sounds more rapidly, uniting them more closely—*bud*. These sounds, so united, form a spoken word. Of what do you think when you hear the word *bud*?

+P+.—I think of a little round thing that grows to be a leafy branch or a flower.

+T+.—Did you see the thing when you were thinking of it?

+P+.—No.

+T+.—Then you must have had a picture of it in your mind. We call this +mental picture+ an +idea+. What called up this idea?

+P+.—It was called up by the word *bud*, which I heard.

+T+.—A *spoken word* then is the sign of what?

+P.—A spoken word is the sign of an idea+.

+T+.—I will call up the same idea in another way. I will *write* three *letters* and unite them thus: *bud*. What do you see?

+P+.—I see the word *bud*.

+T+.—If we call the other word *bud* a *spoken* word, what shall we call this?

+P+.—This is a *written* word.

+T+.—If they stand for the same idea, how do they differ?

+P+.—I *see* this, and I *heard* that.

+T+.—You will observe that we have called attention to *four* different things; viz., the +real bud+; your *mental picture* of the bud, which we have called an +idea+; and the +two words+, which we have called signs of this idea, the one addressed to the ear, and the other to the eye.

+Teacher+.—What did you learn in the previous Lesson?

+Pupil+.—I learned that a spoken word is composed of certain sounds, and that letters are signs of sounds, and that spoken and written words are the signs of ideas.

This question should be passed from one pupil to another till all of these answers are elicited.

All the written words in all the English books ever made, are formed of twenty-six letters, representing about forty sounds. These letters and these sounds make up what is called artificial language.

Of these twenty-six letters, +a, e, i, o, u+, and sometimes +w+ and +y+, are called +vowels+, and the remainder are called +consonants+.

In order that you may understand what kind of sounds the vowels stand for, and what kinds the consonants represent, I will tell you something about the *human voice*.

The air breathed out from your lungs beats against two flat muscles, stretched like strings across the top of the windpipe, and causes them to vibrate. This vibrating makes sound. Take a thread, put one end between your teeth, hold the other in your fingers, draw it tight and strike it, and you will understand how voice is made.

If the voice thus produced comes out through the mouth held well open, a class of sounds is formed which we call *vowel* sounds.

But, if the voice is held back by your palate, tongue, teeth, or lips, *one* kind of *consonant* sounds is made. If the *breath* is driven out *without voice*, and is held back by these same parts of the mouth, the *other* kind of *consonant* sounds is formed. Ex. of both: *b, d, g; p, t, k.*

The teacher and pupils should practice on these sounds till the three kinds can easily be distinguished.

You are now prepared to understand what I mean when I say that the +vowels+ are the +letters+ which stand for the +open sounds of the voice+, and that the +consonants+ are the +letters+ which stand for the sounds made by the +obstructed voice+ and the +obstructed breath+.

The teacher can here profitably spend a few minutes in showing how ideas may be communicated by *Natural Language*, the language of *sighs, groans, gestures* of the hands, *attitudes* of the body, *expressions* of the face, *tones* of the voice, etc. He can show that, in conversation, we sometimes couple this *Natural Language* of *tone* and *gesture* with our language of words, in order to make a stronger impression. Let the pupil be told that, if the passage contain feeling, he should do the same in *Reading* and *Declaiming*.

Let the following definitions be learned, and given at the next recitation.

+DEFINITION.—Artificial Language, or *Language Proper*, consists of the spoken and written words used to communicate ideas and thoughts+.

Let the pupils be required to tell what they learned in the previous lessons.

+Teacher+.—When I pronounce the two words *star* and *bud* thus: *star bud*, how many ideas, or mental pictures, do I call up to you?

+Pupil+.—Two.

+T+.—Do you see any connection between these ideas?

+P+.—No.

+T+.—When I utter the two words *bud* and *swelling*, thus: *bud swelling*, do you see any connection in the ideas they stand for?

+P+.—Yes, I imagine that I see a bud expanding, or growing larger.

+T+.—I will connect two words more closely, so as to express a thought: *Buds swell*. A thought has been formed in my mind when I say, *Buds swell*; and these two words, in which something is said of something else, express that thought, and make what we call a *sentence*. In the former expression, *bud swelling* it is assumed, or taken for granted, that buds perform the act; in the latter, the swelling is asserted as a fact.

Leaves falling. Do these two words express two ideas merely associated, or do they express a thought?

+P+.—They express ideas merely associated.

+T+.—*Leaves fall.*

Same question.

+P+.—A thought.

+T+.—Why?

+P+.—Because, in these words, there is something *said* or *asserted* of leaves.

+T+.—When I say, *Falling leaves rustle*, does *falling* tell what is thought of leaves?

+P+.—No.

+T+.—What does *falling* do?

+P+.—It tells the *kind* of leaves you are thinking and speaking of.

+T+.—What word *does* tell what is thought of leaves?

+P+.—*Rustle.*

+T+.—You see then that in the thought there are two parts; something of which we think, and that which we think about it.

Let the pupils give other examples.

Commit to memory all definitions.

+DEFINITION.—A *Sentence* is the expression of a thought in words+.

Which of the following expressions contain words that have *no connection*, which contain words *merely associated*, and which are *sentences*?

1. Flowers bloom. 2. Ice melts. 3. Bloom ice. 4. Grass grows. 5. Brooks babble. 6. Babbling brooks. 7. Grass soar. 8. Doors open. 9. Open doors. 10. Cows graze. 11. Curling smoke. 12. Sugar graze. 13. Dew sparkles. 14. Hissing serpents. 15. Smoke curls. 16. Serpents hiss. 17. Smoke curling. 18. Serpents sparkles. 19. Melting babble. 20. Eagles soar. 21. Birds chirping. 22. Birds are chirping. 23. Birds chirp. 24. Gentle cows. 25. Eagles are soaring. 26. Bees ice. 27. Working bees. 28. Bees work. 29. Crawling serpents. 30. Landscape piano. 31. Serpents crawl. 32. Eagles clock. 33. Serpents crawling.

REVIEW QUESTIONS.

Illustrate, by the use of *a*, *b*, and *p*, the difference between the *sounds* of letters and their *names*. Letters are the signs of what? What is an idea? A *spoken* word is the sign of what? A *written* word is the sign of what? How do they differ? To what four different things did we call attention in Lesson 1?

How are *vowel* sounds made? How are the two kinds of *consonant* sounds made? What are vowels? Name them. What are consonants? What is artificial language, or language proper? What do you understand by natural language? What is English grammar?

What three kinds of expressions are spoken of in Lessons 3 and 4? Give examples of each. What is a sentence?

ANALYSIS.

On the following sentences, let the pupils be exercised according to the model.

+Model+.—*Intemperance degrades.* Why is this a *sentence?* Ans.—Because it expresses a thought. Of what is something thought? Ans.—Intemperance. Which word tells what is thought? Ans.—*Degrades.*

1. Magnets attract. 2. Horses neigh. 3. Frogs leap. 4. Cold contracts. 5. Sunbeams dance. 6. Heat expands. 7. Sunlight gleams. 8. Banners wave. 9. Grass withers. 10. Sailors climb. 11. Rabbits burrow. 12. Spring advances.

You see that in these sentences there are two parts. The parts are the +Subject+ and the +Predicate+.

+DEFINITION.—The *Subject of a sentence* names that of which something is thought+.

+DEFINITION.—The *Predicate of a sentence* tells what is thought+.

+DEFINITION.—The *Analysis of a sentence* is the separation of it into its parts+.

Analyze, according to the model, the following sentences.

+Model+.—*Stars twinkle*. This is a *sentence*, because it expresses a thought. *Stars* is the *subject*, because it names that of which something is thought; *twinkle* is the *predicate*, because it tells what is thought.

+To the Teacher+.—After the pupils become familiar with the definitions, the "Models" may be varied, and some of the reasons maybe made specific; as, "*Plants* names the things we tell about; *droop* tells what plants do," etc.

Guard against needless repetition.

1. Plants droop. 2. Books help. 3. Clouds float. 4. Exercise strengthens. 5. Rain falls. 6. Time flies. 7. Rowdies fight. 8. Bread nourishes. 9. Boats capsize. 10. Water flows. 11. Students learn. 12. Horses gallop.

ANALYSIS AND THE DIAGRAM.

+Hints for Oral Instruction+.—I will draw on the board a heavy, or shaded, line, and divide it into two parts, thus:

```
              |
===========|============
     |
```

We will consider the first part as the sign of the *subject* of a sentence, and the second part as the sign of the *predicate* of a sentence.

Now, if I write a word over the first line, thus—(doing it)—you will understand that that word is the subject of a sentence. If I write a word over the second line, thus—you will understand that that word is the predicate of a sentence.

The class can see by this picture that *Planets revolve* is a sentence, that *planets* is the subject, and that *revolve* is the predicate.

These signs, or illustrations, made up of straight lines, we call +Diagrams+.

+DEFINITION.+—A *Diagram* is a picture of the offices and relations of the different parts of a sentence+.

Analyze and *diagram* the following sentences.

1. Waves dash. 2. Kings reign. 3. Fruit ripens. 4. Stars shine. 5. Steel tarnishes. 6. Insects buzz. 7. Paul preached. 8. Poets sing. 9. Nero fiddled. 10. Larks sing. 11. Water ripples. 12. Lambs frisk. 13. Lions roar. 14. Tigers growl. 15. Breezes sigh. 16. Carthage fell. 17. Morning dawns. 18. Showers descended. 19. Diamonds sparkle. 20. Alexander conquered. 21. Jupiter thunders. 22. Columbus sailed, 23. Grammarians differ. 24. Cornwallis surrendered.

* * * * *

LESSON 8.

SENTENCE-BUILDING.

You have now learned to analyze sentences, that is, to separate them into their parts. You must next learn to put these parts together, that is, to *build sentences*.

We will find one part, and you must find the other and do the building.

+To the Teacher+.—Let some of the pupils write their sentences on the board, while others are reading theirs. Then let the work on the board be corrected.

Correct any expression that does not make *good sense,* or that asserts something not strictly true; for the pupil should early be taught to *think accurately,* as well as to write and speak grammatically.

Correct all mistakes in *spelling,* and in the use of *capital letters* and the *period.*

Call attention to the agreement in form of the predicate with the subject. See Notes, p. 163.

Insist on neatness. Collect the papers before the recitation closes.

+CAPITAL LETTER-RULE.—The first word of every sentence must begin with a *capital letter*+.

+PERIOD—RULE.—A *period* must be placed after every sentence that simply affirms, denies, or expresses a command+.

Construct sentences by supplying a *subject* to each of the following *predicates*.

Ask yourself the question, What swim, sink, hunt, etc.?

1. —— swim. 2. —— sinks. 3. —— hunt. 4. —— skate. 5. —— jingle. 6. —— decay. 7. —— climb. 8. —— creep. 9. —— run. 10. —— walk. 11. —— snort. 12. —— kick. 13. —— flashes. 14. —— flutters. 15. —— paddle. 16. —— toil. 17. —— terrifies. 18. —— rages. 19. —— expand. 20. —— jump. 21. —— hop. 22. —— bellow. 23. —— burns. 24. —— evaporates.

This exercise may profitably be extended by requiring the pupils to supply *several* subjects to each predicate.

SENTENCE-BUILDING—Continued.

Construct sentences by supplying a *predicate* to each of the following *subjects*.

Ask yourself the question, Artists do what?

1. Artists ——. 2. Sailors ——. 3. Tides ——. 4. Whales ——. 5. Gentlemen ——. 6. Swine ——. 7. Clouds ——. 8. Girls ——. 9. Fruit ——. 10. Powder ——. 11. Hail ——. 12. Foxes ——. 13. Water ——. 14. Frost ——. 15. Man ——. 16. Blood ——. 17. Kings ——. 18. Lilies ——. 19. Roses ——. 20. Wheels ——. 21. Waves ——. 22. Dew ——. 23. Boys ——. 24. Volcanoes ——. 25. Storms ——. 26. Politicians ——. 27. Serpents ——. 28. Chimneys ——. 29. Owls ——. 30. Rivers ——. 31. Nations ——. 32. Indians ——. 33. Grain ——. 34. Rogues ——. 34. Volcanoes ——. 35. Rome ——. 36. Briars ——.

This exercise may be extended by requiring the pupils to supply several predicates to each subject.

REVIEW QUESTIONS.

Of what two parts does a sentence consist? What is the subject of a sentence? What is the predicate of a sentence? What is the analysis of a sentence?

What is a diagram? What rule for the use of capital letters have you learned? What rule for the period?

Impromptu Exercise.

Let the pupils "choose sides," as in a spelling match. Let the teacher select *predicates* from Lesson 8, and give them alternately to the pupils thus arranged. The first pupil prefixes to his word whatever suitable subjects he can think of, the teacher judging of their fitness and keeping the count. This pupil now rises and remains standing until some one else, on his side or the other, shall have prefixed to his word a greater number of apt subjects. The strife is to see who shall be standing at the close of the match, and which side shall have furnished the greater number of subjects. The exercise may be continued with the *subjects* of Lesson 9. Each pupil is to be limited to the same time—one or two minutes.

ANALYSIS.

The +*predicate*+ sometimes contains +*more than one word*+.

Analyze and *diagram* according to the model.

+Model+.—*Socrates was poisoned.*

```
    Socrates | was poisoned
============|================
       |
```

This is a sentence, because it expresses a thought. *Socrates* is the subject, because ——; *was poisoned* is the predicate, because ——. [Footnote: The word *because*—suggesting a reason—should be dropped from these "+Models+" whenever it may lead to mere mechanical repetition.]

1. Napoleon was banished. 2. Andre was captured. 3. Money is circulated. 4. Columbus was imprisoned. 5. Acorns are sprouting. 6. Bells are tolled. 7. Summer has come. 8. Sentences may be analyzed. 9. Clouds are reddening. 10. Air may be weighed. 11. Jehovah shall reign. 12. Corn is planted. 13. Grammarians will differ. 14. Snow is falling. 15. Leaves are rustling. 16. Children will prattle. 17. Crickets are chirping. 18. Eclipses have been foretold. 19. Storms may abate.

SENTENCE-BUILDING.

+To the Teacher+.—Continue oral and written exercises in agreement. See
Notes, pp. 163,164.

Prefix the little helping words in the *second column* to such of the more important words in the *third column* as with them will make complete predicates, and join these predicates to all subjects in the *first column* with which they will unite to make good sense.

```
       1 | 2 | 3
```

Burgoyne | are | woven.
Henry Hudson | was | defeated.
Sparrows | can be | condensed.
Comets | is | inhaled.
Time | have been | worn.
Turbans | may be | slacked.
Lime | has been | wasted.
Steam | could have been | seen.
Air | must have been | deceived.
Carpets | were | quarreling.

Point out the *subject* and the predicate of each sentence in Lessons 28, 31, 34.

Look first for the word that asserts, and then, by putting *who* or *what* before this *predicate*, the *subject* may easily be found.

+To the Teacher+.—Most violations of the rules of concord come from a failure to recognize the relation of subject and predicate when these parts are transposed or are separated by other words. Such constructions should therefore receive special attention. See Notes, pp. 164, 165.

Introduce the class to the Parts of Speech before the close of this recitation. See "Hints for Oral Instruction."

See "Suggestions for COMPOSITION EXERCISES," p. 8, last paragraph.

CLASSES OF WORDS.

+Hints for Oral Instruction+.—By the assistance of the few hints here given, the ingenious teacher may render this usually dry subject interesting and highly attractive. By questioning the pupil as to what he has seen and heard, his interest may be excited and his curiosity awakened.

Suppose that we make an imaginary excursion to some pleasant field or grove, where we may study the habits, the plumage, and the songs of the little birds.

If we attempt to make the acquaintance of every little feathered singer we meet, we shall never get to the end of our pleasant task: but we find that some resemble one another in size, shape, color, habits, and song. These we associate together and call them sparrows.

We find others differing essentially from the sparrows, but resembling one another. These we call robins.

We thus find that, although we were unable to become acquainted with each *individual* bird, they all belong to a few *classes*, with which we may soon become familiar.

It is so with the words of our language. There are many thousand words, all of which belong to eight classes.

These classes of words are called +Parts of Speech+.

We classify birds according to their form, color, etc., but we group words into *classes*, called +Parts of Speech+, with respect to their use in the *sentence*.

We find that many words are names. These we put in one class and call them
+Nouns+.

Each pupil may give the name of something in the room; the name of a distinguished person; a name that may be applied to a class of persons; the name of an animal; the name of a place: the name of a river; the name of a mountain; the name of something which we cannot see or touch, but of which we can think; as, *beauty, mind*.

Remind the pupils frequently that these *names* are all *nouns*.

NOUNS.

+DEFINITION.—A *Noun* is the name of anything+.

Write in columns, headed *nouns*, the names of domestic animals, of garden vegetables, of flowers, of trees, of articles sold in a dry goods store, and of things that cannot be seen or touched; as, *virtue, time, life*.

Write and arrange, according to the following model, the names of things that can *float, fly, walk, work, sit,* or *sing*.

Nouns.

+Model+.—
Cork |
Clouds |
Wood + floats or float.
Ships |
Boys |

Such expressions as *Cork floats* are *sentences,* and the nouns *cork, ship,* etc., are the subjects. You will find that +every subject+ is a +noun+ or some word or words used for a noun.

Be prepared to analyze and parse the sentences which you have made. *Naming the class to which a word belongs is the first step in parsing.*

+Model for Analysis+.—This is a sentence, because ———-; *cork* is the subject, because ———-; *floats* is the predicate, because ———-.

+Parsing+.—*Cork* is a *noun,* because it is the name of a thing—the bark of a tree.

Select and write all the nouns in the sentences given in Lessons 28, 31, 34.

Tell why they are nouns.

In writing the nouns, observe the following rule.

+CAPITAL LETTER—RULE.—Every proper or individual name must begin with a capital letter+.

+To the Teacher+.—See Notes, pp. 167-169.

REVIEW QUESTIONS.

With respect to what, do we classify words (Lesson 14)? What are such classes called? Can you illustrate this classification? What are all names? What is a noun? What is the first step in parsing? What is the rule for writing individual names?

ADJECTIVES.

+Hints for Oral Instruction+.—You are now prepared to consider the *fourth part of speech*. Those words that are added to the subject to modify its meaning are called +Adjectives+.

Some grammarians have formed a separate class of the little words *the*, and *an* or *a*, calling them *articles*.

I will write the word *boys* on the board, and you may name adjectives that will appropriately modify it. As you give them, I will write these adjectives in a column.

Adjectives.

small | large | white | black | straight + boys. crooked | five | some | all |

What words here modify *boys* by adding the idea of size? What by adding the idea of color? What by adding the idea of form? What by adding the idea of number? What are such words called? Why?

Let the teacher name familiar objects and require the pupils to join appropriate adjectives to the names till their stock is exhausted.

+DEFINITION+.—An *Adjective* is a word used to modify a noun or a pronoun+.

Analysis and Parsing.

+Model+.—*A fearful storm was raging*. Diagram and analyze as in Lesson 20.

+Written Parsing+.

Nouns. | *Pronouns.* | *Adjectives.* | *Verbs.* storm | ——— | A fearful | was raging.

+Oral Parsing+.—*A* is an *adjective*, because it is joined to the noun *storm*, to modify its meaning; *fearful* is an *adjective*, because ———; *storm* is a noun, because ———; *was raging* is a verb, because ———-.

1. The rosy morn advances. 2. The humble boon was obtained. 3. An unyielding firmness was displayed. 4. The whole earth smiles. 5. Several subsequent voyages were made. 6. That burly mastiff must be secured. 7. The slender greyhound was released. 8. The cold November rain is falling. 9. That valuable English watch has been sold. 10. I alone have escaped. 11. Both positions can be defended. 12. All such discussions should have been avoided. 13. That dilapidated old wooden building has fallen.

+To the Teacher+.—See Notes, pp. 169, 170.

SENTENCE-BUILDING.

Prefix five adjectives to each of the following nouns.

Shrubs, wilderness, beggar, cattle, cloud.

Write ten sentences with modified subjects, using in each two or more of the following adjectives.

A, an, the, heroic, one, all, many, every, either, first, tenth, frugal, great, good, wise, honest, immense, square, circular, oblong, oval, mild, virtuous, universal, sweet, careless, fragrant.

Write five sentences with modified subjects, each of which shall contain one of the following words as a subject.

Chimney, hay, coach, robber, horizon.

An and *a* are forms of the same word, once spelled *an*, and meaning *one*. After losing something of this force, *an* was still used before vowels and consonants alike; as, *an eagle, an ball, an hair, an use*. Still later, and for the sake of ease in speaking, the word came to have the two forms mentioned above; and an was retained before letters having vowel sounds, but it dropped its *n* and became *a* before letters having consonant sounds. This is the present usage.

CORRECT THESE ERRORS.

A apple; a obedient child; an brickbat; an busy boy.

CORRECT THESE ERRORS.

A heir; a hour; a honor.

Notice, the first letter of these words is *silent*.

CORRECT THESE ERRORS.

An unit; an utensil; an university; an ewe; an ewer; an union; an use; an history; an one.

Unit begins with the sound of the consonant *y*; and *one*, with that of *w*.

+To the Teacher+.—See "Suggestions for COMPOSITION EXERCISES," p. 8, last paragraph.

MODIFIED PREDICATES.

+Hints for Oral Instruction+.—I will now show you how the *predicate* of a sentence may be modified.

The ship sails gracefully. What word is here joined to *sails* to tell the *manner* of sailing? +P+.—*Gracefully.*

+T+.—*The ship sails immediately.* What word is here joined to *sails* to tell the *time* of sailing? +P+.—*Immediately.*

+T+.—*The, ship sails homeward.* What word is here joined to *sails* to tell the *direction* of sailing? +P+.—*Homeward.*

+T+.—These words *gracefully, immediately,* and *homeward* are modifiers of the predicate. In the first sentence, *sails gracefully* is the +Modified Predicate+.

Let the following modifiers be written on the board as the pupil suggests them.

      | instantly.
    | soon.
    | daily.

```
            | hither.
The ship sails + hence.
            | there.
            | rapidly.
            | smoothly.
            | well.
```

Which words indicate the time of sailing? Which, the place? Which, the manner?

The teacher may suggest predicates, and require the pupils to find as many appropriate modifiers as they can.

The Predicate with its modifiers is called the +Modified Predicate+.

Analysis and Parsing.

Analyze and diagram the following sentences, and parse the nouns, pronouns, verbs, and adjectives.

+Model+.—*The letters were rudely carved.*

```
  letters | were carved
=========|===============
\The | \rudely
```

+Written Parsing+.—See *Model*, Lesson 22.

+Oral Analysis+.—This is a sentence, because——; *letters* is the subject, because——; *were carved* is the predicate, because——; *The* is a modifier of the subject, because——; *rudely* is a modifier of the predicate, because

——; *The letters* is the modified subject, *were rudely carved* is the *modified predicate*.

1. He spoke eloquently. 2. She chattered incessantly. 3. They searched everywhere. 4. I shall know presently. 5. The bobolink sings joyously. 6. The crowd cheered heartily. 7. A great victory was finally won. 8. Threatening clouds are moving slowly. 9. The deafening waves dash angrily. 10. These questions may be settled peaceably. 11. The wounded soldier fought bravely. 12. The ranks were quickly broken. 13. The south wind blows softly. 14. Times will surely change. 15. An hour stole on.

ANALYSIS AND PARSING.

ONE MODIFIER JOINED TO ANOTHER.

Analyze and diagram the following sentences, and parse the nouns, pronouns, adjectives, and verbs.

+Model+.—*The frightened animal fled still more rapidly.*

```
           animal | fled
==================|====================
\The \frightened | \rapidly
            \more
             \still
```

+Explanation of the Diagram+.—Notice that the three lines forming this group all slant the same way to show that each stands for a modifying word. The line standing for the principal word of the group is joined to the predicate line. The end of each of the other two lines is broken, and turned to touch its principal at an angle.

+Oral Analysis+.—This is a sentence, because——; *animal* is the subject, because——; *fled* is the predicate, because——; *The* and *frightened* are modifiers of the subject, because——; *still more rapidly* is a modifier of the predicate, because it is a group of words joined to it to limit its meaning; *rapidly* is the principal word of the group; *more* modifies *rapidly,* and *still* modifies *more,* The frightened animal is the modified subject; *fled still more rapidly* is the modified predicate.

1. The crocus flowers very early. 2. A violet bed is budding near. 3. The Quakers were most shamefully persecuted. 4. Perhaps he will return. 5. We laughed very heartily. 6. The yellow poplar leaves floated down. 7. The wind sighs so mournfully. 8. Few men have ever fought so stubbornly. 9. The debt will probably be paid. 10. The visitor will soon be here. 11. That humane project was quite generously sustained. 12. A perfectly innocent man was very cruelly persecuted.

REVIEW QUESTIONS.

What is an adjective? What are the words *an* or *a,* and *the* called by some grammarians? When is *a* used, and when *an?* Give examples of their misuse.

What is the modified predicate? Give an example. Give an example of one modifier joined to another.

Select your subjects from Lesson 9, and construct twenty sentences having modified subjects and modified predicates.

Impromptu Exercise.

Select sentences from Lessons 6, 7, and 11, and conduct the exercise as directed in Lesson 10. Let the strife be to see who can supply the greatest number of modifiers to the subject and to the predicate. The teacher can vary this exercise.

ADVERBS.

+Hints for Oral Instruction+.—You have learned, in the preceding Lessons, that the meaning of the predicate may be limited by modifiers, and that one modifier may be joined to another. Words used to modify the predicate of a sentence and those used to modify modifiers belong to one class, or one *part of speech*, and are called +Adverbs+.

+T+.—*She decided too hastily*. What word tells how she decided? +P+.—-*Hastily*. +T+.—What word tells how hastily? +P+.—*Too*. +T+.—What then are the words *too* and *hastily?* +P+.—Adverbs.

+T+.—*Too much time has been wasted*. What word modifies *much* by telling how much? +P+.—*Too*. +T+.—What *part of speech* is *much?* +P+.—An adjective. +T+.—What then is *too?* +P+.—An adverb.

+T+.—Why is *too* in the first sentence an adverb? Why is *too* in the second sentence an adverb? Why is *hastily* an adverb?

Let the teacher use the following and similar examples, and continue the questions. *He thinks so. So much time has been wasted.*

Let the teacher give verbs, adjectives, and adverbs, and require the pupils to modify them by appropriate adverbs.

+DEFINITION+.—*An Adverb is a word used to modify a verb, an adjective, or an adverb+*.

Analysis and Parsing.

Analyze, diagram, and parse the following sentences.

+Model+.—*We have been very agreeably disappointed.* +Diagram+ as in.
Lesson 25.

For +Written Parsing+, use *Model*, Lesson 22, adding a column for adverbs.

+Oral Parsing+.—*We* is a pronoun, because——; *have been disappointed* is a verb, because——; *very* is an *adverb*, because it is joined to the adverb *agreeably* to tell how agreeably; *agreeably* is an *adverb*, because it is joined to the verb *have been disappointed* to indicate manner.

1. The plough-boy plods homeward. 2. The water gushed forth. 3. Too much time was wasted. 4. She decided too hastily. 5. You should listen more attentively. 6. More difficult sentences must be built. 7. An intensely painful operation was performed. 8. The patient suffered intensely. 9. That story was peculiarly told. 10. A peculiarly interesting story was told. 11. An extravagantly high price was paid. 12. That lady dresses extravagantly.

The pupil will notice that, in some of the examples above, the same adverb modifies an adjective in one sentence and an adverb in another, and that, in other examples, an adjective and a verb are modified by the same word. You may learn from this why such modifiers are grouped into one class.

ANALYSIS AND PARSING.

MISCELLANEOUS EXAMPLES FOR REVIEW.

1. You must diagram neatly. 2. The sheaves are nearly gathered. 3. The wheat is duly garnered. 4. The fairies were called together. 5. The birds chirp merrily. 6. This reckless adventurer has returned. 7. The wild woods rang. 8. White fleecy clouds are floating above. 9. Those severe laws have been repealed. 10. A republican government was established. 11. An unusually large crop had just been harvested. 12. She had been waiting quite patiently. 13. A season so extremely warm had never before been known. 14. So brave a deed [Footnote: *Can be commended* is the verb, and *not* is an adverb.] cannot be too warmly commended.

SENTENCE-BUILDING.

MISCELLANEOUS EXERCISES FOR REVIEW.

Build sentences containing the following adverbs.

Hurriedly, solemnly, lightly, well, how, somewhere, abroad, forever, seldom, exceedingly.

Using the following subjects and predicates as foundations, build six sentences having modified subjects and modified predicates, two of which shall contain adverbs modifying adjectives; two, adverbs modifying adverbs; and two, adverbs modifying verbs.

1. ——— boat glides ———. 2. ——— cloud is rising ———. 3. ——— breezes are blowing ———. 4. ——— elephant was captured ———. 5. ——— streams flow ———. 6. ——— spring has opened ———.

We here give you, in classes, the material out of which you are to build five sentences with modified subjects and modified predicates.

Select the subject and the predicate first.

Nouns and Pronouns. Verbs. Adjectives. Adverbs.

ERRORS FOR CORRECTION.

+To the Teacher+.—We here suggest additional work in composition, with particular reference to the choice and position of adjectives. See Notes, pp. 171,172.

+*Caution*+.—When two or more adjectives are used with a noun, care must be taken in their arrangement. If there is any difference in their relative importance, place nearest the noun the one that is most intimately connected with it.

+To the Teacher+.—We have in mind here those numerous cases where one adjective modifies the noun, and the second modifies the noun as limited by the first. *All ripe apples are picked.* Here *ripe* modifies *apples*, but *all* modifies *apples* limited by *ripe*. Not *all apples* are *picked*, but only *all* that are *ripe*.

CORRECT THE FOLLOWING ERRORS OF POSITION.

A wooden pretty bowl stood on the table.
The blue beautiful sky is cloudless.
A young industrious man was hired.
The new marble large house was sold.

+Caution+.—When the adjectives are of the *same* rank, place them where they will sound the best. This will usually be in the order of length—the longest last.

CORRECT THESE ERRORS.

An entertaining and fluent speaker followed.
An enthusiastic, noisy, large crowd was addressed.

+Caution+.—Do not use the pronoun +them+ for the adjective +those+.

CORRECT THESE ERRORS.

Them books are nicely bound.
Them two sentences should be corrected.

CORRECT THE FOLLOWING MISCELLANEOUS ERRORS.

arouse, o romans
hear, o israel
it is i
i may be Mistaken
you Have frequently been warned
some Very savage beasts have been Tamed

REVIEW QUESTIONS.

What is an adverb? Give an example of an adverb modifying an adjective; one modifying a verb; one modifying an adverb. Why are such expressions as *a wooden pretty bowl* faulty? Why is *an enthusiastic, noisy, large crowd* faulty? Why is *them books* wrong? Why is *i may be Mistaken* wrong? Why is *hear, o israel,* wrong? Study the Review Questions given in previous Lessons.

PHRASES INTRODUCED BY PREPOSITIONS.

+Hints for Oral Instruction+.—In the preceding Lessons, you have learned that several words may be grouped together and used as one modifier. In the examples given, the principal word is joined directly to the subject or to the predicate, and this word is modified by another word. In this Lesson also groups of words are used as modifiers, but these words are not united with one another, or with the word which the group modifies, just as they are in the preceding Lessons. I will write on the board this sentence: *De Soto marched into Florida.* +T+.—What tells where De Soto marched? +P+.—*Into Florida.* +T+.—What is the principal word of the group? +P+.—*Florida.* +T+.—Is *Florida* joined directly to the predicate, as rapidly was in Lesson 25? +P+.—No. +T+.—What little word comes in to unite the modifier to *marched?* +P+.—*Into.* +T+.—Does *Florida* alone, tell where he marched? +P+.—No. +T+.—Does *into* alone, tell where he marched? +P+.—No.

+T+.—These groups of related words are called +Phrases+. Let the teacher draw on the board the diagram of the sentence above.

Phrases of the form illustrated in this diagram are the most common, and they perform a very important function in our language.

Let the teacher frequently call attention to the fact that all the words of a phrase are *taken together* to perform *one distinct office*.

A phrase modifying the subject is equivalent to an adjective, and, frequently, may be changed into one. *The dew of the morning has passed away*. What word may be used for the phrase *of the morning*? +P+.—*Morning*. +T+.—Yes. The *morning* dew has passed away.

A phrase modifying the predicate is equivalent to an adverb, and, frequently, may be changed into one. *We shall go to that place*. What word may be used for the phrase, *to that place*? +P+.—*There*. +T+.—Yes. We shall go *there*.

Change the phrases in these sentences:—

_A citizen of America was insulted.

We walked toward home_.

Let the teacher write on the board the following words, and require the pupils to add to each, one or more words to complete a phrase, and then to construct a sentence in which the phrase may be properly employed: *To, from, by, at, on, with, in, into, over*.

+DEFINITION.—A *Phrase* is a group of words denoting related ideas but not expressing a thought+.

Analysis and Parsing.

Analyze the following sentences, and parse the nouns, pronouns, adjectives, verbs, and adverbs.

Model.—*The finest trout in the lake are generally caught in the deepest water.*

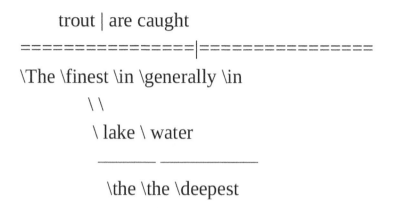

+Explanation of the Diagram+.—You will notice that the diagram of the *phrase* is made up of a slanting line, standing for the introductory and connecting word, and a horizontal line, representing the principal word. Under the latter, are placed the little slanting lines standing for the modifiers of the principal word. Here and elsewhere all modifiers are joined to their principal words by slanting lines.

+Oral Analysis+.—This is a sentence, because ———; *trout* is the subject, because ———; *are caught* is the predicate, because ———; the words *The* and *finest*, and the phrase, *in the lake*, are modifiers of the subject, because ———; the word *generally* and the phrase, *in the deepest water*, are modifiers of the predicate, because ———; *in* introduces the first phrase, and *lake* is the principal word; *in* introduces the second phrase, and *water* is the principal word; *the* and *deepest* are modifiers of *water*; *The finest trout in the lake* is the modified subject, and *are generally caught in the deepest water* is the modified predicate.

1. The gorilla lives in Africa. 2. It seldom rains in Egypt. 3. The Pilgrims landed at Plymouth. 4. The wet grass sparkled in the light. 5. The little brook ran swiftly under the bridge. 6. Burgoyne surrendered at Saratoga. 7. The steeples of the village pierced through the dense fog.

SENTENCE-BUILDING.

Build sentences, employing the following phrases as modifiers.

To Europe, of oak, from Albany, at the station, through the fields, for vacation, among the Indians, of the United States.

Supply to the following predicates subjects modified by phrases.

—— is situated on the Thames. —— has arrived. —— was destroyed by an earthquake. —— was received. —— has just been completed. —— may be enjoyed.

Supply to the following subjects predicates modified by phrases.

Iron ——.
The trees ——.
Squirrels ——.
The Bible ——.
Sugar ——.
Cheese ——.
Paul ——.
Strawberries ——.
The mountain ——.

SENTENCE-BUILDING.

Re-write the following sentences, changing the italicized words into equivalent phrases.

+Model+.—A *golden* image was made.
An image *of gold* was made.

You will notice that the adjective *golden* was placed before the subject, but, when changed to a phrase, it followed the subject.

1. The book was *carefully* read. 2. The old soldiers fought *courageously*. 3. A group of children were strolling *homeward*. 4. No season of life should be spent *idly*. 5. The *English* ambassador has just arrived. 6. That *generous* act was liberally rewarded.

Change the following adjectives and adverbs into equivalent phrases, and employ the phrases in sentences of your own building.

Wooden, penniless, eastward, somewhere, here, evening, everywhere, yonder, joyfully, wintry.

Make a sentence out of the words in each line below.

PREPOSITIONS.

+Hints for Oral Instruction+.—In the preceding Lessons, the little words that were placed before nouns, thus forming phrases, belong to a, class of words called +Prepositions+. You noticed that these words, which you have now learned to call prepositions, served to introduce phrases. The preposition shows the relation of the *idea* expressed by the principal word of the phrase to that of the word which the phrase modifies. It serves also to connect these words.

In the sentence, *The squirrel ran up a tree*, what word shows the relation of the act of running, to the tree? Ans. *Up*.

Other words may be used to express different relations. Repeat, nine times, the sentence above given, supplying, in the place of *up*, each of the following prepositions: *Around, behind, down, into, over, through, to, under, from*.

Let this exercise be continued, using such sentences as, *The man went into the house; The ship sailed toward the bay*.

+DEFINITION.—A *Preposition* is a word that introduces a phrase modifier, and shows the relation, in sense, of its principal word to the word modified+.

+Analysis and Parsing+.

+Model+.—*Flowers preach to us.*

For +Analysis+ and +Diagram+, see Lesson 31.

For +Written Parsing+, see Lesson 22. Add the needed columns.

+Oral Parsing+.—*Flowers* is a noun, because——; *preach* is a verb, because——; *to* is a *preposition*, because it shows the relation, in sense, between *us* and *preach; us* is a pronoun, because it is used instead of the name of the speaker and the names of those for whom he speaks.

1. The golden lines of sunset glow. 2. A smiling landscape lay before us. 3. Columbus was born at Genoa. 4. The forces of Hannibal were routed by Scipio. 5. The capital of New York is on the Hudson. 6. The ships sail over the boisterous sea. 7. All names of the Deity should begin with capital letters. 8. Air is composed chiefly of two invisible gases. 9. The greater portion of South America lies between the tropics. 10. The laurels of the warrior must at all times be dyed in blood. 11. The first word of every entire sentence should begin with a capital letter. 12. The subject of a sentence is generally placed before the predicate.

Impromptu Exercise.

(The teacher may find it profitable to make a separate lesson of this exercise.)

COMPOUND SUBJECT AND COMPOUND PREDICATE.

When two or more subjects united by a connecting word have the same predicate, they form a +Compound Subject;+ and, when two or more predicates connected in like manner have the same subject, they form a +Compound Predicate+.

In the sentence, *Birds and bees can fly*, the two words *birds* and *bees*, connected by *and*, have the same predicate; the same action is asserted of both birds and bees. In the sentence, *Leaves fade and fall*, two assertions are made of the same things. In the first sentence, *birds* and *bees* form the *compound subject*; and, in the second, *fade* and *fall* form the *compound predicate*.

Analyze and parse the following sentences.

+Models+.—*Napoleon rose, reigned, and fell.*

Frogs, antelopes, and kangaroos can jump.

```
                rose Frogs
     ,=,===== ======.=.
     / ' ' \
Napoleon| / X ' reigned antelopes ' X \ | can jump
```

```
========|==| '======== ==========' |==|=========
    | \and' 'and/ |
      \ ' fell kangaroos ' /
       `_'====== ==========':='
```

+Explanation of the Diagram+.—The short line following the subject line represents the entire predicate, and is supposed to be continued in the three horizontal lines that follow, each of which represents one of the parts of the *compound predicate*. These three lines are united by dotted lines, which stand for the connecting words. The +X+ denotes that an *and* is understood.

Study this explanation carefully, and you will understand the other diagram.

+Oral Analysis+ of the first sentence.

This is a sentence, because ——; *Napoleon* is the subject, because ——; *rose, reigned,* and *fell* form the *compound predicate*, because they belong in common to the same subject, and say something about Napoleon. *And* connects *reigned* and *fell*.

1. The Rhine and the Rhone rise in Switzerland. 2. Time and tide wait for no man. 3. Washington and Lafayette fought for American Independence. 4. Wild birds shrieked, and fluttered on the ground. 5. The mob raged and roared. 6. The seasons came and went. 7. Pride, poverty, and fashion cannot live in the same house. 8. The tables of stone were cast to the ground and broken. 9. Silver or gold will be received in payment. 10. Days, months, years, and ages will circle away.

CONJUNCTIONS AND INTERJECTIONS.

The words *and* and *or*, used in the preceding Lesson to connect the nouns and the verbs, belong to a class of words called +*Conjunctions*+.

Conjunctions may also connect *words* used as *modifiers*; as,

A daring *but* foolish feat was performed.

They may connect phrases; as,

We shall go to Saratoga *and* to Niagara.

They may connect *clauses*, that is, expressions that, standing alone, would be sentences; as,

He must increase, *but* I must decrease.

+DEFINITION.—A *Conjunction*, is a word used to connect words, phrases, or clauses+.

The +*Interjection*+ is the eighth and last *part of speech*. Interjections are mere exclamations, and are without grammatical relation to any other word in the sentence.

+DEFINITION+.—An *Interjection* is a word used to express strong or sudden feeling+.

Examples:—

Bravo! hurrah! pish! hush! ha, ha! alas! hail! lo! pshaw!

Analyze and parse the following sentences.

+Model+.—*Hurrah! that cool and fearless fireman has rushed into the house and up the burning stairs.*

```
    Hurrah
   _____


    fireman | has rushed
===================|========================
\That\ and \ | \ and \
    \.....\ \........\
     \ \ \ \up
      \cool \fearless \into \stairs
                   _____
                    \house \the \burning
                            _____
                             \the
```

+Explanation of the Diagram+.—The line representing the interjection is not connected with the diagram. Notice the dotted lines, one standing for the *and* which connects the two *word* modifiers; the other, for the *and* connecting the two *phrase* modifiers.

+Written Parsing+.

N.	Pro.	Adj.	Vb.	Adv.	Prep.	Conj.	Int.
fireman	the		has rushed into		and		
house	that				up and		hurrah
stairs		cool					
		fearless					
		burning					

+Oral Parsing+ of the *conjunction* and the *interjection*.

The two *ands* are conjunctions, because they *connect*. The first connects two word modifiers; the second, two phrase modifiers. *Hurrah* is an *interjection*, because it expresses a burst of sudden feeling.

1. The small but courageous band was finally overpowered. 2. Lightning and electricity were identified by Franklin. 3. A complete success or an entire failure was anticipated. 4. Good men and bad men are found in all communities. 5. Vapors rise from the ocean and fall upon the land. 6. The Revolutionary war began at Lexington and ended at Yorktown. 7. Alas! all hope has fled. 8. Ah! I am surprised at the news. 9. Oh! we shall certainly drown. 10. Pshaw! you are dreaming. 11. Hurrah! the field is won.

PUNCTUATION AND CAPITAL LETTERS.

+COMMA—RULE.—Phrases that are placed out of their natural order [Footnote: A phrase in its natural order follows the word it modifies.] and made emphatic, or that are loosely connected with the rest of the sentence, should be set off by the comma+.

PUNCTUATE THE FOLLOWING SENTENCES.

+Model+.—The cable, *after many failures*, was successfully laid. Upon the platform 'twixt eleven and twelve I'll visit you. To me this place is endeared by many associations. Your answers with few exceptions have been correctly given. In English much depends on the placing of phrases.

+COMMA—RULE.—Words or phrases connected by conjunctions are separated from each other by the comma unless all the conjunctions are expressed+.

PUNCTUATE THE FOLLOWING SENTENCES.

+Model+.—Caesar *came, saw, and conquered.*
　　Caesar *came and saw and conquered.*

He travelled in *England, in Scotland, and in Ireland.*

(The comma is used in the first sentence, because a conjunction is omitted; but not in the second, as all the conjunctions are expressed.)

A brave prudent and honorable man was chosen.

Augustus Tiberius Nero and Vespasian were Roman emperors.

Through rainy weather across a wild country over muddy roads after a long ride we came to the end of our journey.

+PERIOD and CAPITAL LETTER—RULE.—*Abbreviations* generally begin with capital letters and are always followed by the period+.

CORRECT THE FOLLOWING ERRORS.
+Model.—+*Mr., Esq., N. Y., P. M.*

gen, a m, mrs, no, u s a, n e, eng, p o, rev, prof, dr, gram, capt, coi, co, va, conn.

+EXCLAMATION POINT—RULE.—All *exclamatory expressions* must be followed by the exclamation point+.

PUNCTUATE THE FOLLOWING EXPRESSIONS.

+Model.—+*Ah! Oh! Zounds! Stop pinching!*

Pshaw, whew, alas, ho Tom, halloo Sir, good-bye, welcome.

SENTENCE-BUILDING.

+To the Teacher.—+Call attention to the agreement of verbs with compound subjects. Require the pupils to justify the verb-forms in Lesson 36 and elsewhere. See Notes, pp. 165-167.

Write *predicates* for the following *compound subjects*.

Snow and hail; leaves and branches; a soldier or a sailor; London and Paris.

Write *compound predicates* for the following *subjects*.

The sun; water; fish; steamboats; soap; farmers; fences; clothes.

Write *subjects* for the following *compound predicates*.

Live, feel, and grow; judges and rewards; owes and pays; inhale and exhale; expand and contract; flutters and alights; fly, buzz, and sting; restrain or punish.

Write *compound subjects* before the following *predicates*.

SENTENCE-BUILDING.

Supply *attribute complements* to the following expressions. (See Caution, Lesson 40.)

The marble feels ——. Mary looks ——. The weather continues ——. The apple tastes ——. That lady appears ——. The sky grows ——. The leaves of roses are ——. The undertaking was pronounced ——.

Write a subject and a predicate to each of the following nouns taken as *attribute complements*.

+Model+.—*Soldier*.—That old man has been a *soldier*.

Plant, insect, mineral, vegetable, liquid, gas, solid, historian, poet, artist, traveler, emperor.

Using the following nouns as subjects, build sentences each having a simple predicate and two or more *object complements*.

Congress, storm, education, king, tiger, hunter, Arnold, shoemakers, lawyers, merchant.

Build three sentences on each of the following subjects, two of which shall contain *object complements*, and the third, an *attribute complement*.

SUBJECT OR COMPLEMENT MODIFIED BY A PARTICIPLE.

+Hints for Oral Instruction+.—You have learned, in the preceding Lessons, that a *quality* may be *assumed* as belonging to a thing; as, *white chalk*, or that it may be *asserted* of it; as, *Chalk is white*. An *action*, also, may be *assumed* as belonging to something; as, *Peter turning*, or it may be *asserted;* as, Peter *turned*. In the expression, *Peter, turning, said*, what word expresses an action as *assumed,* and which *asserts* an action? Each pupil may give an example of an action asserted and of an action assumed; as, Corn *grows*, corn *growing*; geese *gabble*; geese *gabbling*.

This form of the verb, which merely *assumes* the act, being, or state, is called the +Participle+.

When the words *growing* and *gabbling* are placed before the nouns, thus: *growing corn, gabbling geese*, they tell simply the kind of corn and the kind of geese, and are therefore *adjectives*.

When *the* or some other adjective is placed before these words, and a preposition after them, thus: *The growing of the corn, the gabbling of the geese*, they are simply the *names* of actions, and are therefore *nouns*.

Let each pupil give an example of a verb asserting an action, and change it to express:—

1st, An *assumed* action; 2d, A permanent *quality;* 3d, The *name* of an action.

Participles may be completed by *objects* and *attributes*.

+Analysis and Parsing+.

+Model+.—*Truth, crushed to earth, will rise again.*

```
    Truth | will rise
==========|==============
 \cru | \again
  \ shed
  _____

    \to
     \ earth
      _____-
```

+Explanation of the Diagram+.—In this diagram, the line standing for the principal word of the participial phrase is broken; one part slants, and the other is horizontal. This shows that the participle *crushed* is used like an adjective to modify *Truth*, and yet retains the nature of a verb, expressing an action received by truth.

+Oral Analysis+.—This is a sentence, because ——; *Truth* is the subject, because ——; *will rise* is the predicate, because ——; the phrase, *crushed to earth*, is a modifier of the Subj., because ——; *crushed* introduces the phrase and is the principal word in it; the phrase *to earth* is a modifier of *crushed*; *to* introduces it, and *earth* is the principal word in it; *again* is a modifier of the Pred., because ——. *Truth crushed to earth* is the modified subject, *will rise again* is the modified predicate.

+Parsing+—*Crushed* is the form of the verb called *participle*. The action expressed by it is merely *assumed*.

1. The mirth of Addison is genial, imparting a mild glow of thought. 2. The general, riding to the front, led the attack. 3. The balloon, shooting swiftly into the clouds, was soon lost to sight. 4. Wealth acquired dishonestly will prove a curse. 5. The sun, rising, dispelled the mists. 6. The thief, being detected, surrendered to the officer. 7. They boarded the vessel lying in the harbor. 8. The territory claimed by the Dutch was called New Netherlands. 9. Washington, having crossed the Delaware, attacked the Hessians stationed at Trenton. 10. Burgoyne, having been surrounded at Saratoga, surrendered to Gen. Gates. 11. Pocahontas was married to a young Englishman named John Rolfe. 12. A shrug of the shoulders, translated into words, loses much force. 13. The armies of England, mustered for the battles of Europe, do not awaken sincere admiration.

(Note that the participle, like the predicate verb, may consist of two or more words.)

(Note, too, that the participle, like the adjective, may belong to a *noun complement*.)

THE INFINITIVE PHRASE.

+Hints for Oral Instruction+.—There is another form of the verb which, like the participle, cannot be the predicate of a sentence, for it cannot *assert*; as, She went out *to see* a friend; *To lie* is a disgrace. As this form of the verb expresses the action, being, or state in a general manner, without limiting it directly to a subject, it is called an +Infinitive+, which means *without limit*. The infinitive generally follows *to*; as, *to walk, to sleep*.

Let each pupil give an infinitive.

The infinitive and the preposition *to* constitute a phrase, which may be employed in several ways.

+T+.—*I have a duty to perform*. The infinitive phrase modifies what?

+P+.—The noun *duty*. +T+.—It then performs the office of what? +P+.—Of an adjective modifier.

+T+.—*I come to hear*. The infinitive phrase modifies what? +P+.—The verb *come*. +T+.—What office then does it perform? +P+.—Of an adverb modifier.

+T+.—*To lie is base. What* is base? +P+.—*To lie.* +T+.—*He attempted to speak. What* did he attempt? +P+.—*To speak.* +T+.—*To lie* is a subject, and *to speak* is an *object*. What part of speech is used as subject and object? +P+.—The noun.

+T+.—The +Infinitive+ phrase is used as an +adjective+, an +adverb+, and a +noun+.

Infinitives may be completed by *objects* and *attributes*.

+Analysis and Parsing+.

+Model+.—*David hasted to meet Goliath.*

```
    David | hasted
==========|===========
     | \to
         \ meet | Goliath
           \————————————
```

+Analysis of the Infinitive Phrase+.—*To* introduces the phrase; *meet*, completed by the object *Goliath*, is the principal part.

+Parsing of the Phrase+.—*To* is a preposition, because ——; *meet* is a verb, because ——; *Goliath* is a noun, because ——.

1. I come not here to talk. 2. I rejoice to hear it. 3. A desire to excel leads to eminence. 4. Dr. Franklin was sent to France to solicit aid for the colonies. 5. To retreat was impossible.

(*To* is here used merely to introduce the infinitive phrase.)

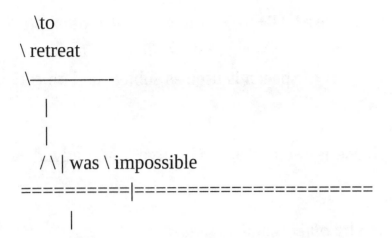

+Explanation of the Diagram+.—As this *phrase subject* cannot, in its proper form, be written on the subject line, it is placed above, and, by means of a support, the phrase diagram is made to rest on the subject line. The *phrase complement* may be diagramed in a similar way, and made to rest on the complement line.

6. The hands refuse to labor. 7. To live is not all of life. 8. The Puritans desired to obtain religious freedom. 9. The Romans, having conquered the world, were unable to conquer themselves. 10. Narvaez sailed from Cuba to conquer Florida. 11. Some savages of America and Africa love to wear rings in the nose. 12. Andrew Jackson, elected to succeed J. Q. Adams, was inaugurated in 1829.

POSITION AND PUNCTUATION OF THE PARTICIPIAL PHRASE.

ERRORS TO BE CORRECTED. (See Caution 1, Lesson 41.)

Punctuate as you correct. (See Lesson 37.)

A house was built for a clergyman having seven gables.
The old man struck the saucy boy raising a gold-headed cane.
We saw a marble bust of Sir W. Scott entering the vestibule.
Here is news from a neighbor boiled down.
I found a cent walking over the bridge.
Balboa discovered the Pacific ocean climbing to the top of a mountain.

Punctuate the following exercises.

Cradled in the camp Napoleon was the darling of the army.
Having approved of the plan the king put it into execution.
Satan incensed with indignation stood unterrified.
My friend seeing me in need offered his services.
James being weary with his journey sat down on the wall.
The owl hid in the tree hooted through the night.

REVIEW QUESTIONS.

Give the caution relating to the position of the phrase modifier; that relating to the choice of prepositions; that relating to the double negative (Lesson 41). Give examples of errors. Can a noun be an attribute complement? Illustrate. What do you understand by a participle? Into what may some participles be changed? Illustrate. What offices does the infinitive phrase perform? Illustrate them.

+To the Teacher+.—See COMPOSITION EXERCISES in the Supplement—Selection from George Eliot.

REVIEW.

MISCELLANEOUS ERRORS FOR CORRECTION. (See Cautions in Lessons 30, 40, and 41.)

There never was such another man.
He was an old venerable patriarch.

John has a cadaverous, hungry, and lean look.
He was a well-proportioned, fine fellow.

Pass me them potatoes.

Put your trust not in money.
We have often occasion for thanksgiving,

Now this is to be done how?
Nothing can justify ever profanity.

To continually study is impossible.

(An adverb is seldom placed between the preposition *to* and the infinitive.)

Mary likes to tastefully dress.
Learn to carefully choose your words.

She looks queerly.
Give me a soon and direct answer.

The post stood firmly.
The eagle flies highly.
The orange tastes sweetly.

I feel tolerable well.
The branch breaks easy.
Thistles grow rapid.
The eagle flies swift.
This is a miserable poor pen.

A wealthy gentleman will adopt a little boy with a small family.
A gentleman called from Africa to pay his compliments.

Water consists in oxygen and hydrogen.
He went out attended with a servant.
I have a dislike to such tricksters.
We have no prejudice to foreigners.
She don't know nothing about it.
Father wouldn't give me none.
He hasn't been sick neither.
I won't have no more nohow.

+To the Teacher+.—Let the reason be given for every correction.

SENTENCE-BUILDING.

Build sentences in which the following participles shall be used as modifiers.

Being fatigued; laughing; being amused; having been elected; running; having been running.

Expand each of the following sentences into three sentences, using the *participial form* of the verb as a *participle*, in the first; the same form as an *adjective*, in the second; and as a *noun*, in the third.

+Model+.—The stream *flows*. The stream, *flowing* gently, crept through the meadow. The *flowing* stream slipped away to the sea. The *flowing* of the stream caused a low murmur. The stream flows. The sun rises. Insects hum. The birds sing. The wind whistles. The bells are ringing. The tide ebbs.

Form *infinitive phrases* from the following verbs, and use these phrases as *adjectives, adverbs,* and *nouns,* in sentences of your own building.

Smoke, dance, burn, eat, lie, try.

+To the Teacher+.—For exercises to distinguish the participle from the predicate verb, see Notes, pp. 181, 182.

NOUNS AND PRONOUNS AS MODIFIERS.

+Hints for Oral Instruction+.—In the sentence, *The robin's eggs are blue,* the noun *robin's* does what? +P+.—It tells what or whose eggs are blue. +T+.—What word names the things owned or possessed? +P+.—*Eggs.* +T+.—What word names the owner or possessor? +P+.—*Robin's.*

+T+.—The noun *robin's* is here used as a *modifier*. You see that this word, which I have written on the board, is the word *robin* with a little mark (') called an apostrophe, and the letter *s* added. These are added to denote possession.

In the sentence, *Webster, the statesman, was born in New Hampshire,* the noun *statesman* modifies the subject *Webster* by explaining what or which Webster is meant. Both words name the same person.

Let the pupils give examples of each of these two kinds of +Noun Modifiers+—the +Possessive+ and the +Explanatory+.

Analysis and Parsing.

+Model+.—*Julia's sister Mary has lost her diamond ring.*

```
    sister (Mary) | has lost | ring
===============|============'=============
 \Julia's |      \her \diamond
```

+Explanation of the Diagram+.—*Mary* is written on the subject line, because *Mary* and *sister* both name the same person, but the word *Mary* is inclosed within marks of parenthesis to show that *sister* is the proper grammatical subject.

In *oral analysis*, call *Julia's* and *Mary* modifiers of the subject, *sister*, because *Julia's* tells whose sister, and *Mary* explains sister by adding another name of the same person. *Her* is a modifier of the object, because it tells whose ring is meant.

Julia's sister Mary is the *modified subject*, the predicate is unmodified, and *her diamond ring* is the *modified object complement*.

1. The planet Jupiter has four moons. 2. The Emperor Nero was a cruel tyrant. 3. Peter's wife's mother lay sick of a fever.

```
    mother
  ========
  \wife's
   \Peter's
```

4. An ostrich outruns an Arab's horse. 5. His pretty little nephew Arthur had the best claim to the throne. 6. Milton, the great English poet, became blind. 7. Caesar gave his daughter Julia in marriage to Pompey. 8. London, the capital of England, is the largest and richest city in the world. 9. Joseph, Jacob's favorite son, was sold by his brethren to the Ishmaelites. 10. Alexander the Great [Footnote: *Alexander the Great* may be taken as one name, or *Great* may be called an explanatory modifier of *Alexander*.]

SENTENCE-BUILDING.

Nouns and pronouns denoting possession may generally be changed to equivalent phrases; as, *Arnold's treason* = *the treason of Arnold*. Here the preposition *of* indicates *possession*, the same relation expressed by the apostrophe (') and *s*. Change the following possessive nouns to equivalent phrases, and the phrases indicating possession to possessive nouns, and then expand the expressions into complete sentences.

+Model+.—The *earth's* surface. The surface *of the earth* is made up of land and water.

The earth's surface: Solomon's temple; England's Queen; Washington's Farewell Address; Dr. Kane's Explorations; Peter's wife's mother; George's friend's father; Shakespeare's plays; Noah's dove; the diameter of the earth; the daughter of Jephthah; the invasion of Burgoyne; the voyage of Cabot; the Armada of Philip; the attraction of the earth; the light of the moon.

Find for the things mentioned below, *other* names which shall describe or explain them. Add such names to these nouns, and then expand the expressions into complete sentences.

+Model+.—*Ink.*—*Ink, a dark fluid,* is used in writing.

Observe the following rule.

+COMMA-RULE.+—An *Explanatory Modifier*, when it does not restrict the modified term or combine closely with it, is set off by the comma+.

+To the Teacher+.—See Notes, pp. 176, 177.

New York, rain, paper, the monkey, the robin, tea, Abraham Lincoln, Alexander Hamilton, world, peninsula, Cuba, Shakespeare.

Write three sentences, each of which shall contain a noun or pronoun denoting possession, and a noun or pronoun used to explain.

+To the Teacher+.—For additional exercises in the use of possessive modifiers, see Notes, pp. 182, 183.

ANALYSIS AND PARSING.

MISCELLANEOUS EXAMPLES IN REVIEW.

1. The toad spends the winter in a dormant state. 2. Pride in dress or in beauty betrays a weak mind. 3. The city of London is situated on the river Thames. 4. Napoleon Bonaparte was born in 1769, on an island in the Mediterranean. 5. Men's opinions vary with their interests. 6. Ammonia is found in the sap of trees, and in the juices of all vegetables. 7. Earth sends up her perpetual hymn of praise to the Creator. 8. Having once been deceived by him, I never trusted him again. 9. Aesop, the author of Aesop's Fables, was a slave. 10. Hope comes with smiles to cheer the hour of pain. 11. Clouds are collections of vapors in the air. 12. To relieve the wretched was his pride. 13. Greece, the most noted country of antiquity, scarcely exceeded in size the half of the state of New York.

ANALYSIS AND PARSING.

MISCELLANEOUS EXAMPLES IN REVIEW—CONTINUED.

1. We are never too old to learn. 2. Civility is the result of good nature and good sense. 3. The right of the people to instruct their representatives is generally admitted. 4. The immense quantity of matter in the Universe presents a most striking display of Almighty power. 5. Virtue, diligence, and industry, joined with good temper and prudence, must ever be the surest means of prosperity. 6. The people called Quakers were a source of much trouble to the Puritans. 7. The Mayflower brought to America [Footnote: One hundred and one may be taken as one adjective.] one hundred and one men, women, and children. 8. Edward Wingfield, an avaricious and unprincipled man, was the first president of the Jamestown colony. 9. John Cabot and his son Sebastian, sailing under a commission from Henry VII. of England, discovered the continent of America. 10. True worth is modest and retiring. 11. Jonah, the prophet, preached to the inhabitants of Nineveh.

COMPLEX SENTENCES.

THE ADJECTIVE CLAUSE.

+Hints for Oral Instruction+.—A word-modifier may sometimes be expanded into a phrase or into an expression that asserts.

+T+.—*A wise man will be honored*. Expand *wise* into a phrase, and give me the sentence. +P+.—A man *of wisdom* will be honored. +T+.—Expand *wise* into an expression that asserts, join this to *man*, as a modifier, and then give me the entire sentence. +P+.—A man *who is wise* will be honored.

+T+.—You see that the same quality may be expressed in three ways—A *wise* man, A man *of wisdom*, A man *who is wise*.

Let the pupils give similar examples.

+T+.—In the sentence, *A man who is wise will be honored,* the word *who* stands for what? +P+.—For the noun *man*. +T+.—Then what part of speech is it? +P+.—A pronoun.

+T+.—Put the noun *man* in the place of the pronoun *who*, and then give me the sentence. +P+.—*A man, man is wise, will be honored.*

+T+.—I will repeat your sentence, changing the order of the words—*A man will be honored. Man is wise.* Is the last sentence now joined to the first as a modifier, or are they two separate sentences? +P+.—They are two separate sentences.

+T+.—Then you see that the pronoun *who* not only stands for the noun *man*, but it connects the modifying expression, *who is wise*, to *man*, the subject of the sentence, *A man will be honored*, and thus there is formed what we call a +Complex Sentence+. These two parts we call +Clauses+. *A man will be honored* is the +Independent Clause;+ *who is wise* is the +Dependent Clause+.

Clauses that modify nouns or pronouns are called +Adjective Clauses+.

+DEFINITION.—A *Clause* is a part of a sentence containing a subject and its predicate+.

+DEFINITION.—A *Dependent Clause* is one used as an adjective, an adverb, or a noun+.

+DEFINITION.—An *Independent Clause* is one not dependent on another clause+.

+DEFINITION.—A *Simple Sentence* is one that contains but one subject and one predicate, either or both of which may be compound+.

+DEFINITION.—A *Complex Sentence* is one composed of an independent clause and one or more dependent clauses+.

Analysis and Parsing.

+Model+.—

```
        man | will be honored
========|==================
\A `|
      `
        `
    who `| is \ wise
    ———-|————
         |
```

+Explanation of the Diagram+.—You will notice that the lines standing for the subject and predicate of the *independent clause* are heavier than those of the *dependent clause*. This pictures to you the relative importance of the two clauses. You will see that the pronoun *who* is written on the subject line of the dependent clause. But this word performs the office of a conjunction also, and this office is expressed in the diagram by a dotted line. As all modifiers are joined by *slanting* lines, to the words they modify, you learn from this diagram that *who is wise* is a modifier of *man*.

+Oral Analysis+.—This is a *complex sentence*, because it consists of an *independent clause* and a *dependent clause*. *A man will be honored* is *the independent clause*; *who is wise* is the *dependent clause*. *Man* is the subject of the independent clause; *will be honored* is the predicate. The word *A* and the clause, *who is wise*, are modifiers of the subject. *A* points out *man*, and *who is wise* tells the *kind* of man. *A man who is wise* is the modified subject; the predicate is unmodified. *Who* is the subject of the dependent clause, *is* is the predicate, and *wise* is the attribute complement. *Who* connects the two clauses.

1. He that runs may read. 2. Man is the only animal that laughs and weeps. 3. Henry Hudson discovered the river which bears his name. 4. He necessarily remains weak who never tries exertion. 5. The meridians are

those lines that extend from pole to pole. 6. He who will not be ruled by the rudder must be ruled by the rock. 7. Animals that have a backbone are called vertebrates. 8. Uneasy lies the head that wears a crown. 9. The thick mists which prevail in the neighborhood of Newfoundland are caused by the warm waters of the Gulf Stream. 10. The power which brings a pin to the ground holds the earth in its orbit. 11. Death is the black camel which kneels at every man's gate. 12. Our best friends are they who tell us of our faults, and help us to mend them.

The pupil will notice that, in some of these sentences, the dependent clause modifies the subject, and that, in others, it modifies the noun complement.

+COMMA—RULE.—The *adjective* or the *adverb clause*, when it does not closely follow and restrict the word modified, is generally set off by the comma+.

SENTENCE-BUILDING.

ADJECTIVE CLAUSES.

Expand each of the following adjectives into

1. A phrase; 2. A clause;

and then use these three modifiers in three separate sentences of your own construction.

+Model+.—*Energetic; of energy;* + or | *who has energy,*
| *who is energetic.*

An *energetic* man will succeed. A man *of energy* will succeed. A man who has *energy* (or *who is energetic*) will succeed.

Honest, long-eared, beautiful, wealthy.

Expand each of the following *possessive nouns* into

1. A phrase; 2. A clause;

and then use these three modifiers in three separate sentences.

+Model+.—*Saturn's rings*; the rings *of Saturn*; the rings *which surround Saturn*.

Saturn's rings can be seen with a telescope. The *rings of Saturn* can be seen with a telescope. The rings *which surround Saturn* can be seen, with a telescope.

Absalom's hair; the hen's eggs; the elephant's tusks.

Change the following simple sentences into complex sentences by expanding the participial phrases into clauses.

The vessels carrying the blood from the heart are called arteries. The book prized above all other books is the Bible. Rivers rising west of the Rocky Mts. flow into the Pacific ocean. The guns fired at Concord were heard around the world.

+To the Teacher+.—For additional composition exercises with particular reference to adjective clauses, see Notes, p. 177.

COMPLEX SENTENCES.

THE ADVERB CLAUSE.

+Hints for Oral Instruction+.—You learned in Lesson 83 that an adverb can be expanded into an equivalent phrase; as, The book was *carefully* read = The book was read *with care*.

We shall now learn that a phrase used as an adverb may be expanded into an +Adverb clause+. In the sentence, *We started at sunrise,* what phrase is used like an adverb? +P+.—*At sunrise.* +T+.—Expand this phrase into an equivalent clause, and give me the entire sentence. +P+.—We started *when the sun rose*.

+T+.—You see that the phrase, *at sunrise,* and the clause, *when the sun rose,* both modify *started,* telling the time of starting, and are therefore equivalent to adverbs. We will then call such clauses +Adverb Clauses+.

Analysis and Parsing.

+Model.—+

```
    We | started
=========|=============
```

```
      \
    ` when
  sun \ rose
 =======|=========
  \the
```

+Explanation of the Diagram+.—The line which connects the two predicate lines pictures three things. It is made up of three parts. The upper part shows that *when* modifies *started*; the lower part, that it modifies *rose*; and the dotted part shows that it *connects*.

+Oral Analysis+.—This is a complex sentence, because ———; *We started* is the independent clause, and *when the sun rose* is the dependent clause. *We* is the subject of the independent clause, and *started* is the predicate. The clause, *when the sun rose*, is a modifier of the predicate, because it tells when we started. *Started when the sun rose* is the modified predicate.

Sun is the subject of the dependent clause, and *rose* is the predicate, and *the* is a modifier of *sun*; *the sun* is the modified subject. *When* modifies *rose* and *started*, and connects the clause-modifier to the predicate *started*.

+Parsing+ of *when*.—*When* is an adverb modifying the two verbs *started* and *rose*, thus connecting the two clauses. It modifies these verbs by showing that the two actions took place at the same time.

1. The dew glitters when the sun shines. 2. Printing was unknown when Homer wrote the Iliad. 3. Where the bee sucks honey, the spider sucks poison. 4. Ah! few shall part where many meet. 5. Where the devil cannot come, he will send. 6. While the bridegroom tarried, they all slumbered and slept. 7. Fools rush in where angels fear to tread. 8. When the tale of bricks is doubled, Moses comes. 9. When I look upon the tombs of the great, every emotion of envy dies within me. 10. The upright man speaks as he thinks.

SENTENCE-BUILDING.

ADVERB CLAUSES.

Expand each of the following phrases into an adverb clause, and fit this clause into a sentence of your own building.

+Model+.—*At sunset; when the sun set.* We returned *when the sun set.*

At the hour; on the playground; by moonlight; in youth; among icebergs; after school; at the forks of the road; during the day; before church; with my friend.

To each of the following independent clauses, join an adverb clause, and so make complex sentences.

—— Peter began to sink. The man dies ——. Grass grows ——. Iron —— can easily be shaped. The rattlesnake shakes his rattle ——. —— a nation mourns. Pittsburg stands ——. He dared to lead ——.

+To the Teacher+.—For additional composition exercises with particular reference to adverb clauses, see Notes, p. 177.

See COMPOSITION EXERCISES in the Supplement—Selection from the Brothers

Grimm.

REVIEW QUESTIONS.

In what two ways may nouns be used as modifiers? Illustrate. Nouns and pronouns denoting possession may sometimes be changed into what? Illustrate. Give the rule for the punctuation of explanatory modifiers. Into what may an adjective be expanded? Into what may a participial phrase be expanded? Give illustrations. Give an example of a complex sentence. Of a clause. Of an independent clause. Of a dependent clause. Into what may a phrase used as an adverb be expanded? Illustrate.

THE NOUN CLAUSE.

+Hints for Oral Instruction+.—*That stars are suns is taught by astronomers*. What is taught by astronomers? +P+.—That stars are suns. +T+.—What then is the subject of *is taught*? +P+.—The clause, *That stars are suns*. +T+.—This clause then performs the office of what part of speech? +P+.—Of a noun.

+T+.—*Astronomers teach that stars are suns*. What do astronomers teach?
+P+.—That stars are suns. +T+.—What is the object complement of *teach*? +P+.—The clause, *that stars are suns*. +T+.—What office then does this clause perform? +P+.—That of a noun.

+T+.—*The teaching of astronomers is, that stars are suns*. What does *is* assert of teaching? +P+.—That stars are suns. +T+.—What then is the attribute complement? +P+.—*That stars are suns*. +T+.—Does this complement express the quality of the subject, or does it name the same thing that the subject names? +P+.—It names the same thing that the subject names. +T+.—It is equivalent then to what part of speech? +P+.—To a noun.

+T+.—You see then that a clause, like a noun, may be used as the subject or the complement of a sentence.

Analysis and Parsing.

+Model+.—

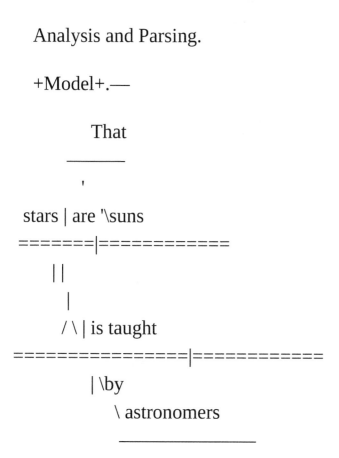

You will understand this diagram from the explanation of the second diagram in Lesson 49.

+Oral Analysis+.—This is a complex sentence, in which the whole sentence takes the place of the independent clause. *That stars are suns* is the dependent clause. *That stars are suns* is the subject of the whole sentence, etc. ——. *That* simply introduces the dependent clause.

In *parsing*, call *that* a conjunction.

1. That the Scotch are an intelligent people is generally acknowledged. 2. That the moon is made of green cheese is believed by some boys and girls.

3. That Julius Caesar invaded Britain is a historic fact. 4. That children should obey their parents is a divine precept. 5. I know that my Redeemer liveth. 6. Plato taught that the soul is immortal. 7. Peter denied that he knew his Lord. 8. Mahomet found that the mountain would not move. 9. The principle maintained by the colonies was, that taxation without representation is unjust. 10. Our intention is, that this work shall be well done. 11. Our hearts' desire and prayer is, that you may be saved. 12. The belief of the Sadducees was, that there is no resurrection of the dead.

* * * * *

LESSON 62.

COMPOUND SENTENCES.

ANALYSIS AND PARSING.

+DEFINITION.—A *Compound Sentence* is one composed of two or more independent clauses+.

+Model+.—*War has ceased, and peace has come.*

```
    War | has ceased
=======|=============
      | '
       ' and
       '.....
          '
  peace | has ' come
========|===============
       |
```

+Explanation of the Diagram+.—These two clause diagrams are shaded alike to show that the two clauses are of the same rank. The connecting line is not slanting, for one clause is not a modifier of the other. As one entire clause is connected with the other, the connecting line is drawn between the predicates simply for convenience.

+Oral Analysis+.—This is a *compound sentence,* because it is made up of two independent clauses. The first clause, etc. ——.

1. Morning dawns, and the clouds disperse. 2. Prayer leads the heart to God, and he always listens. 3. A soft answer turneth away wrath, but grievous words stir up anger. 4. Power works easily, but fretting is a perpetual confession of weakness. 5. Many meet the gods, but few salute them. 6. We eat to live, but we do not live to eat. 7. The satellites revolve in orbits around the planets, and the planets move in orbits around the sun. 8. A wise son maketh a glad father, but a foolish son is the heaviness of his mother. 9. Every man desires to live long, but no man would be old. 10. [Footnote: A verb is to be supplied in each of the last three sentences.] Pride goeth before destruction, and a haughty spirit before a fall. 11. Towers are measured by their shadows, and great men, by their calumniators. 12. Worth makes the man, and want of it, the fellow.

SENTENCES CLASSIFIED WITH RESPECT TO THEIR MEANING.

+Hints for Oral Instruction+.—You have already become acquainted with three kinds of sentences. Can you name them?

+P+.—The Simple sentence, the Complex, and the Compound.

+T+.—These classes have been made with regard to the *form* of the sentence. We will now arrange sentences in classes with regard to their *meaning*.

Mary sings. Does Mary sing? Sing, Mary. How Mary sings! Here are four simple sentences. Do they all *mean* the same thing?

+P+.—They do not.

+T+.—Well, you see they differ. Let me tell you wherein. The first one tells a fact, the second asks a question, the third expresses a command, and the fourth expresses sudden thought or strong feeling. We call the first a +Declarative sentence+, the second an +Interrogative sentence+, the third an +Imperative sentence+, and the fourth an +Exclamatory sentence+.

+DEFINITION.—A *Declarative Sentence* is one that is used to affirm or to deny+.

+DEFINITION+.—An *Interrogative Sentence* is one that expresses a question+.

+DEFINITION+.—An *Imperative Sentence* is one that expresses a command or an entreaty+.

+DEFINITION+.—An *Exclamatory Sentence* is one that expresses sudden thought or strong feeling+.

+INTERROGATION POINT—RULE.+—Every direct interrogative sentence should be followed by an interrogation point+. [Footnote: To The Teacher.—See Notes, pp. 178, 179.]

SENTENCE-BUILDING.

Change each of the following declarative sentences into three interrogative sentences, and tell how the change was made.

+Model+.—*Girls can skate. Can girls skate? How can girls skate? What girls can skate?* You are happy. Parrots can talk. Low houses were built.

Change each of the following into an imperative sentence. Notice that independent words are set off by the comma.

+Model+.—*Carlo eats his dinner. Eat your dinner, Carlo.* George plays the flute. Birdie stands on one leg.

Change each of the following into exclamatory sentences.

+Model+.—*You are happy. How happy you are! What a happy child you are!*
You are so happy!

CLASSES OF ADJECTIVES.

+Hints for Oral Instruction+.—When I say *large, round, sweet, yellow oranges*, the words *large, round, sweet,* and *yellow* modify the word *oranges* by telling the *kind,* and limit the application of the word to oranges of that kind.

When I say *this orange, yonder orange, one orange,* the words *this, yonder,* and *one* do not tell the kind, but simply point out or number the orange, and limit the application of the word to the orange pointed out or numbered.

Adjectives of the first class describe by giving a quality, and so are called +Descriptive adjectives+.

Adjectives of the second class define by pointing out or numbering, and so are called +Definitive adjectives+.

Let the teacher write nouns on the board, and require the pupils to modify them by appropriate descriptive and definitive adjectives.

DEFINITIONS.

+A *Descriptive Adjective* is one that modifies by expressing quality+.

+A *Definitive Adjective* is one that modifies by pointing out, numbering, or denoting quantity+.

SENTENCE-BUILDING.

Place the following adjectives in two columns, one headed *descriptive*, and the other *definitive*, then build simple sentences in which they shall be employed as *modifiers*. Find out the meaning of each word before you use it.

Round, frolicsome, first, industrious, jolly, idle, skillful, each, the, faithful, an, kind, one, tall, ancient, modern, dancing, mischievous, stationary, nimble, several, slanting, parallel, oval, every.

Build simple sentences in which the following *descriptive* adjectives shall be employed as *attribute complements*. Let some of these attributes be *compound*.

Restless, impulsive, dense, rare, gritty, sluggish, dingy, selfish, clear, cold, sparkling, slender, graceful, hungry, friendless.

Build simple sentences in which the following *descriptive* adjectives shall be employed.

Some of these adjectives have the *form* of *participles*, and some are *derived* from *proper nouns*.

+CAPITAL LETTER—RULE.—An Adjective derived from a proper noun must begin with a capital letter+.

Shining, moving, swaying, bubbling, American, German, French, Swiss, Irish, Chinese.

CLASSES OF VERBS.

+Hints for Oral Instruction+.—*The man caught* makes no complete assertion, and is not a sentence. If I add the object complement *fish*, I complete the assertion and form a sentence—*The man caught fish*. The action expressed by *caught* passes over from the man to the fish. *Transitive* means *passing over*, and so all those verbs that express an action that passes over from a doer to something which receives, are called +Transitive verbs+.

Fish swim. The verb *swim* does not require an object to complete the sentence. No action passes from a doer to a receiver. These verbs which express action that does not pass over to a receiver, and all those which do not express action at all, but simply *being* or *state of being*, are called +Intransitive verbs+.

Let the teacher write transitive and intransitive verbs on the board, and require the pupils to distinguish them.

When I say, I *crush* the worm, I express an action that is going on now, or in present time. I *crushed* the worm, expresses an action that took place in past time. As *tense* means *time*, we call the form *crush* the *present tense* of the verb, and *crushed* the *past tense*. In the sentence, The worm *crushed* under my foot died, *crushed,* expressing the action as assumed, is, as you have already learned, a participle; and, as the action is completed, we call it a *past participle.* Now notice that *ed* was added to *crush,* the verb in the present tense, to form the verb in the past tense, and to form the past participle. Most verbs form their past tense and their past participle by adding *ed,* and so we call such +Regular verbs+.

I *see* the man; I *saw* the man; The man *seen* by me ran away. I *catch* fish in the brook; I *caught* fish in the brook; The fish *caught* in the brook tasted good. Here the verbs *see* and *catch* do not form their past tense and past participle by adding *ed* to the present, and so we call them *Irregular verbs.*

Let the teacher write on the board verbs of both classes, and require the pupils to distinguish them.

DEFINITIONS.

CLASSES OF VERBS WITH RESPECT TO MEANING.

+A *Transitive Verb* is one that requires an object+. [Footnote: The *object* of a transitive verb, that is, the name of the receiver of the action, may be the *object complement,* or it may be the subject; as, Brutus stabbed *Caesar, Caesar* was stabbed by Brutus.]

+An *Intransitive Verb* is one that does not require an object+.

CLASSES OF VERBS WITH RESPECT TO FORM.

+A *Regular Verb* is one that forms its past tense and past participle by adding *ed* to the present+. [Footnote: If the present ends in *e,* the *e* is dropped when *ed* is added; as, lov_e_, lov_ed_; believ_e_, believ_ed_.]

+An *Irregular Verb* is one that does not form its past tense and past participle by adding *ed* to the present+.

SENTENCE-BUILDING.

Place the following verbs in two columns, one headed *transitive* and the other, *intransitive*. Place the same verbs in two other columns, one headed *regular* and the other, *irregular*. Build these verbs into sentences by supplying a subject to each intransitive verb, and a subject and an object to each transitive verb.

Vanish, gallop, bite, promote, contain, produce, provide, veto, secure, scramble, rattle, draw.

Arrange the following verbs as before, and then build them into sentences by supplying a subject and a noun attribute to each intransitive verb, and a subject and an object to each transitive verb.

Degrade, gather, know, was, became, is.

A verb may be transitive in one sentence and intransitive in another. Use the following verbs both ways.

+Model+.—The wren *sings* sweetly.

The wren *sings* a pretty little song.

Bend, ring, break, dash, move.

CLASSES OF ADVERBS.

+Hints for Oral Instruction+.—When I say, He will come *soon*, or *presently*, or *often*, or *early*, I am using, to modify *will come*, words which express the *time* of coming. These and all such adverbs we call +Adverbs of Time+.

He will come *up*, or *hither*, or *here*, or *back*. Here I use, to modify *will come*, words which express *place*. These and all such adverbs we call +Adverbs of Place+.

When I say, The weather is *so* cold, or *very* cold, or *intensely* cold, the words *so, very,* and *intensely* modify the adjective *cold* by expressing the *degree* of coldness. These and all such adverbs we call +Adverbs of Degree+.

When I say, He spoke *freely, wisely,* and *well*, the words *freely, wisely,* and *well* tell how or *in what manner* he spoke. All such adverbs we call +Adverbs of Manner+.

Let the teacher place adverbs on the board, and require the pupil to classify them.

DEFINITIONS.

+*Adverbs of Time* are those that generally answer the question+, *When?*

_+Adverbs of Place are those that generally answer the question+, Where?

+Adverbs of Degree are those that generally answer the question+, To what extent?

+Adverbs of Manner are those that generally answer the question+, In what way?_

SENTENCE-BUILDING.

Place the following adverbs in the four classes we have made—if the classification be perfect, there will be five words in each column—then build each adverb into a simple sentence.

Partly, only, too, wisely, now, here, when, very, well, where, nobly, already, seldom, more, ably, away, always, not, there, out.

Some adverbs, as you have already learned, modify two verbs, and thus connect the two clauses in which these verbs occur. Such adverbs are called +*Conjunctive Adverbs*+.

The following *dependent* clauses are introduced by *conjunctive adverbs*. Build them into complex sentences by supplying *independent clauses*.

——— *when* the ice is smooth; ——— *while* we sleep; ——— *before* winter comes; ——— *where* the reindeer lives; ——— *wherever* you go.

CLASSES OF CONJUNCTIONS. [Footnote: For classified lists, see pp. 190,191.]

+Hints for Oral Instruction+.—*Frogs, antelopes, and kangaroos can jump.* Here the three nouns are of the same rank in the sentence. All are subjects of *can jump. War has ceased, and peace has come.* In this compound sentence, there are two clauses of the same rank. The word *and* connects the subjects of *can jump*, in the first sentence: and the two clauses, in the second. All words that connect words, phrases, or clauses of the *same rank* are called +Co-ordinate Conjunctions+.

If you have tears, prepare to shed them now. I will go, because you need me. Here *if* joins the clause, *you have tears*, as a modifier, expressing condition, to the independent clause, *prepare to shed them now;* and *because* connects *you need me,* as a modifier, expressing reason or cause, to the independent clause, *I will go.* These and all such conjunctions as connect dependent clauses to clauses of a *higher rank* are called +Subordinate Conjunctions+.

Let the teacher illustrate the meaning and use of the words *subordinate* and *co-ordinate*.

DEFINITIONS.

+*Co-ordinate Conjunctions* are such as connect words, phrases, or clauses of the same rank+.

+*Subordinate Conjunctions* are such as connect clauses of different rank+.

SENTENCE-BUILDING.

Build four short sentences for each of the three *co-ordinate conjunctions* that follow. In the first, let the conjunction be used to connect principal parts of a sentence; in the second, to connect word modifiers; in the third, to connect phrase modifiers; and in the fourth, to connect independent clauses.

And, or, but.

Write four short complex sentences containing the four *subordinate conjunctions* that follow. Let the first be used to introduce a noun clause, and the other three to connect adverb clauses to independent clauses.

That, for, if, because.

REVIEW QUESTIONS.

What new subject begins with page 95? Name and define the different classes of nouns. Illustrate by examples the difference between common nouns and proper nouns. Name and define the different classes of pronouns. Can the pronoun *I* be used to stand for the one spoken to?—the one spoken of? Does the relative pronoun distinguish by its *form* the speaker, the one spoken to, and the one spoken of? Illustrate. Can any other class of pronouns be used to connect clauses?

For what do interrogative pronouns stand? Illustrate. Where may the antecedent of an interrogative pronoun generally be found? *Ans.—The antecedent of an interrogative pronoun may generally lie found in the answer to the question.*

Name and define the different classes of adjectives. Give an example of each class. Name and define the different classes of verbs, made with respect to their meaning. Give an example of each class. Name and define the different classes of verbs, made with respect to their form. Give an example of each class.

Name and define the different classes of adverbs. Give examples of each kind. Name and define the different classes of conjunctions. Illustrate by examples.

Are prepositions and interjections subdivided? (See "Schemes" for the conjunction, the preposition, and the interjection, p. 188.)

+To the Teacher+.—See COMPOSITION EXERCISES in the Supplement— Selection from Dr. John Brown.

We suggest that other selections from literature be made and these exercises continued.

MODIFICATIONS OF THE PARTS OF SPEECH.

NOUNS AND PRONOUNS.

You have learned that two words may express a thought, and that the thought may be varied by adding modifying words. You are now to learn that the meaning or use of a word may sometimes be changed by simply changing its *form*. The English language has lost many of its inflections, or forms, so that frequently changes in the meaning and use of words are not marked by changes in form. These *changes* in the *form*, *meaning*, and *use* of the parts of speech, we call their +Modifications+.

The boy shouts. The boys shout. I have changed the form of the subject *boy* by adding an *s* to it. The meaning has changed. *Boy* denotes *one* lad; *boys*, *two or more* lads. This change in the form and meaning of nouns is called +Number+. The word *boy*, denoting one thing, is in the +Singular Number;+ and *boys*, denoting more than one thing, is in the +Plural Number+.

Let the teacher write other nouns on the board, and require the pupils to form the plural of them.

DEFINITIONS.

+*Modifications of the Parts of Speech* are changes in their form, meaning, and use+.

NUMBER.

+*Number* is that modification of a noun or pronoun which denotes one thing or more than one+.

+The *Singular Number* denotes one thing+.

+The *Plural Number* denotes more than one thing+.

+RULE.—The *plural* of nouns is regularly formed by adding *s* to the singular+.

Write the plural of the following nouns.

Tree, bird, insect, cricket, grasshopper, wing, stick, stone, flower, meadow, pasture, grove, worm, bug, cow, eagle, hawk, wren, plough, shovel.

When a singular noun ends in the sound of *s*, *x*, *z*, *sh*, or *ch*, it is not easy to add the sound of *s*, so *es* is added to make another syllable.

Write the plural of the following nouns.

Guess, box, topaz, lash, birch, compass, fox, waltz, sash, bench, gas, tax, adz, brush, arch.

Many nouns ending in *o* preceded by a consonant form the plural by adding *es* without increasing the number of syllables.

Write the plural of the following nouns.

Hero, cargo, negro, potato, echo, volcano, mosquito, motto.

Common nouns ending in *y* preceded by a consonant form the plural by changing *y* into *i* and adding *es* without increasing the number of syllables.

Write the plural of the following nouns.

Lady, balcony, family, city, country, daisy, fairy, cherry, study, sky.

Some nouns ending in *f* and *fe* form the plural by changing *f* or *fe* into *ves* without increasing the number of syllables.

Write the plural of the following nouns.

Sheaf, loaf, beef, thief, calf, half, elf, shelf, self, wolf, life, knife, wife.

NUMBER.

From the following list of nouns, select, and write in separate columns: 1st. Those that have no plural; 2d. Those that have no singular; 3d. Those that are alike in both numbers.

Pride, wages, trousers, cider, suds, victuals, milk, riches, flax, courage, sheep, deer, flour, idleness, tidings, thanks, ashes, scissors, swine, heathen.

The following nouns have very irregular plurals. Learn to spell the plurals.

Singular. Plural. Singular. Plural.
Man, men. Foot, feet.
Woman, women. Ox, oxen.
Child, children. Tooth, teeth.
Mouse, mice. Goose, geese.

Learn the following plurals and compare them with the groups in the preceding Lesson.

NOUNS AND PRONOUNS.—GENDER.

+Hints for Oral Instruction+.—*The lion was caged. The lioness was caged*. In the first sentence, something was said about a *male* lion; and in the second, something was said about a *female* lion. Modifications of the noun to denote the sex of the object, we call +Gender+. Knowing the sex of the object, you know the gender of its name. The word *lion*, denoting a male animal, is in the +Masculine Gender;+ and *lioness*, denoting a female lion, is in the +Feminine Gender+.

The names of things *without* sex are in the +Neuter Gender+.

Such words as *cousin, child, friend, neighbor*, may be *either masculine or feminine*.

+DEFINITIONS.

Gender is that modification of a noun or pronoun which denotes sex.

The *Masculine Gender* denotes the male sex.

The *Feminine Gender* denotes the female sex.

The *Neuter Gender* denotes want of sex+.

The masculine is distinguished from the feminine in three ways:—

1st. By a difference in the ending of the nouns.

2d. By different words in the compound names.

3d. By words wholly or radically different.

Arrange the following pairs in separate columns with reference to these ways.

Abbot, abbess; actor, actress; Francis, Frances; Jesse, Jessie; bachelor, maid; beau, belle; monk, nun; gander, goose; administrator, administratrix; baron, baroness; count, countess; czar, czarina; don, donna; boy, girl; drake, duck; lord, lady; nephew, niece; landlord, landlady; gentleman, gentlewoman; peacock, peahen; duke, duchess; hero, heroine; host, hostess; Jew, Jewess; man-servant, maid-servant; sir, madam; wizard, witch; marquis, marchioness; widow, widower; heir, heiress; Paul, Pauline; Augustus, Augusta.

REVIEW QUESTIONS.

What new way of varying the meaning of words is introduced in Lesson 78? Illustrate. What are modifications of the parts of speech? What is number? How many numbers are there? Name and define each. Give the rule for forming the plural of nouns. Illustrate the variations of this rule. What is gender? How many genders are there? Name and define each. In how many ways are the genders distinguished? Illustrate.

NOUNS AND PRONOUNS.—PERSON AND CASE.

+Hints for Oral Instruction+.—*Number* and *gender*, as you have already learned, are modifications affecting the *meaning* of nouns and pronouns. Number is almost always indicated by the ending; gender, sometimes. There are two other modifications which refer not to changes in the *meaning* of nouns and pronouns, but to their different *uses* and *relations*. In the English language, these changes are not often indicated by a change of *form*.

I Paul have written. *Paul, thou* art beside thyself. *He* brought *Paul* before Agrippa. In these three sentences the word *Paul* has *three different uses*. In the first, it is used as the name of the *speaker*; in the second, as the name of *one spoken to*; in the third, as the name of *one spoken of*. You will notice that the *form* of the noun was not changed. This change in the use of nouns and pronouns is called +Person+. The word *I* in the first sentence, the word *thou* in the second, and the word *he* in the third have each a different use. *I, thou,* and *he* are personal pronouns, and, as you have learned, distinguish *person* by their *form*. *I*, denoting the speaker, is in the +First Person+; *thou*, denoting the one spoken to, is in the +Second Person+; and *he*, denoting the one spoken of, is in the +Third Person+.

Personal pronouns and *verbs* are the only words that distinguish person by their form.

The bear killed the man. The man killed the bear. The bear's grease was made into hair oil. In the first sentence, the bear is represented as *performing* an action; in the second, as *receiving* an action; in the third, as *possessing* something. So the word *bear* in these sentences has three different uses. These uses of nouns are called +Cases+. The use of a noun as subject is called the +Nominative Case+; its use as object is called the +Objective Case+; and its use to denote possession is called the +Possessive Case+.

The *possessive* is the only case of nouns that is indicated by a change in *form*.

A noun or pronoun used as an *attribute* complement is in the *nominative case*. A noun or pronoun following a preposition as the principal word of a phrase is in the *objective case*. *I* and *he* are *nominative* forms. *Me* and *him* are *objective* forms.

The following sentences are therefore incorrect: It is *me*; It is *him*; *Me* gave the pen to *he*.

+DEFINITIONS.+

Person is that modification of a noun or pronoun which denotes the speaker, the one spoken to, or the one spoken of.

The *First Person* denotes the one speaking.

The *Second Person* denotes the one spoken to.

The *Third Person* denotes the one spoken of.

Case is that modification of a noun or pronoun which denotes its office in the sentence.

The *Nominative Case of a noun or pronoun* denotes its office as subject or as attribute complement.

The *Possessive Case of a noun or pronoun* denotes its office as possessive modifier.

The *Objective Case of a noun or pronoun* denotes its office as object complement, or as principal word in a prepositional phrase+.

NOUNS AND PRONOUNS.—PERSON AND CASE.

Tell the *person* and *case* of each of the following nouns and pronouns.

+Remember+ that a noun or pronoun used as an *explanatory modifier* is in the same case as the word which it explains, and that a noun or pronoun used *independently* is in the *nominative case*.

We Americans do things in a hurry.
You Englishmen take more time to think.
The Germans do their work with the most patience and deliberation.
We boys desire a holiday.
Come on, my men; I will lead you.
I, your teacher, desire your success.
You, my pupils, are attentive.
I called on Tom, the tinker.
Friends, countrymen, and lovers, hear me for my cause.

Write simple sentences in which each of the following nouns shall be used in the *three persons* and in the *three cases*.

Andrew Jackson, Alexander, Yankees.

Write a sentence containing a noun in the *nominative* case, used as an *attribute;* one in the *nominative,* used as an *explanatory modifier;* one in the *nominative,* used independently.

Write a sentence containing a noun in the *objective case,* used to *complete two predicate verbs;* one used to *complete* a *participle;* one used to *complete* an *infinitive;* one used *with a preposition* to make a phrase; one used as an *explanatory modifier*.

+To the Teacher+.—See pp. 183, 184.

NOUNS AND PRONOUNS.—DECLENSION.

+DEFINITION.—*Declension* is the arrangement of the cases of nouns and pronouns in the two numbers+.

Declension of Nouns.

LADY.

Singular. *Plural*. *Nom*. lady, ladies, *Pos*. lady's, ladies', *Obj*. lady; ladies.

CHILD.

Singular. *Plural*. *Nom*. child, children, *Pos*. child's, children's, *Obj*. child; children.

Declension of Pronouns.

PERSONAL PRONOUNS.

FIRST PERSON.

Singular. *Plural*. *Nom*. I, we, *Pos*. my *or* mine, our *or* ours, *Obj*. me; us.

SECOND PERSON—*common form.*

> *Singular. Plural. Nom.* you, you, *Pos.* your *or* yours, your *or* yours, *Obj.* you; you.

SECOND PERSON—*old form.*

> *Singular. Plural. Nom.* thou, ye or you, *Pos.* thy *or* thine, your *or* yours, *Obj.* thee; you.

THIRD PERSON—*masculine.*

> *Singular. Plural. Nom.* he, they, *Pos.* his, their *or* theirs, *Obj.* him; them.

THIRD PERSON—*feminine.*

> *Singular. Plural. Nom.* she, they, *Pos.* her *or* hers, their *or* theirs, *Obj.* her; them.

THIRD PERSON——*neuter.*

> *Singular. Plural. Nom.* it, they, *Pos.* its, their *or* theirs, *Obj.* it; them.

Mine, ours, yours, thine, hers, and *theirs* are used when the name of the thing possessed is omitted; as, This rose is *yours* = This rose is *your rose.*

COMPOUND PERSONAL PRONOUNS.

By joining the word *self* to the possessive forms *my, thy, your,* and to the objective forms *him, her, it,* the +Compound Personal Pronouns+ are formed. They have no possessive case, and are alike in the nominative and the objective.

Their plurals are *ourselves, yourselves,* and *themselves*. Form the *compound personal pronouns,* and write their declension.

RELATIVE AND INTERROGATIVE PRONOUNS.

Sing. and Plu. Nom. who, *Pos.* whose, *Obj.* whom.

Sing. and Plu. Nom. which, *Pos.* whose, *Obj.* which.

Of which is often used instead of the possessive form of the latter pronoun.

Sing. and Plu. Nom. that, *Pos.* ——, *Obj.* that.

Sing. and Plu. Nom. what, *Pos.* ——, *Obj.* what.

Ever and *soever* are added to *who, which,* and *what* to form the +Compound Relative Pronouns+. They are used when the antecedent is omitted. For declension, see above.

POSSESSIVE FORMS.

+RULE.—The *possessive case* of nouns is formed in the singular by adding to the nominative the apostrophe and the letter *s* ('s); in the plural, by adding (') only. If the plural does not end in *s*, the apostrophe and the *s* are both added+.

Write the *possessive singular* and the *possessive plural* of the following nouns, and place an appropriate noun after each.

Robin, friend, fly, hero, woman, bee, mouse, cuckoo, fox, ox, man, thief,
 fairy, mosquito, wolf, shepherd, farmer, child, neighbor, cow.

Possession may be expressed also by the preposition *of* and the *objective*; as, the *mosquito's* bill = the bill *of* the *mosquito*.

The possessive sign ('s) is confined *chiefly* to the names of persons and animals.

We do not say the *chair's* legs, but the legs *of* the *chair*. Regard must be had also to the *sound*.

IMPROVE THE FOLLOWING EXPRESSIONS, and expand each into a simple sentence.

The sky's color; the cloud's brilliancy; the rose's leaves; my uncle's partner's house; George's father's friend's farm; the mane of the horse of my brother; my brother's horse's mane.

When there are several possessive nouns, all belonging to one word, the possessive sign is added to the last only. If they modify different words, the sign is added to each.

CORRECT THE FOLLOWING EXPRESSIONS, and expand each into a simple sentence.

+Model+.—*Webster and Worcester's dictionary may be bought at Ticknor's and Field's book-store.*

The possessive sign should be added to *Webster,* for the word *dictionary* is understood immediately after. Webster and Worcester do not together possess the same dictionary. The sign should not be added to *Ticknor,* for the two men, Tieknor and Field, possess the same store.

Adam's and Eve's garden; Jacob's and Esau's father; Shakespeare and Milton's works; Maud, Kate, and Clara's gloves; Maud's, Kate's, and Clara's teacher was ———.

When one possessive noun is explanatory of another, the possessive sign is added to the last only.

CORRECT THE FOLLOWING ERRORS.

I called at Tom's the tinker's.
They listened to Peter's the Hermit's eloquence.

FORMS OF THE PRONOUN.

+Remember+ that *I, we, thou, ye, he, she, they,* and *who* are +nominative+ forms, and must not be used in the objective case.

+Remember+ that *me, us, thee, him, her, them,* and *whom* are +objective+ forms, and must not be used in the nominative case.

+To the Teacher+.—The *eight* nominative forms and the *seven* objective forms given above are the only distinctive nominative and objective forms in the English language. Let the pupils become familiar with them.

CORRECT THE FOLLOWING ERRORS.

Him and me are good friends.
The two persons were her and me.
Us girls had a jolly time.
It is them, surely.
Who will catch this? Me.
Them that despise me shall be lightly esteemed.
Who is there? Me.
It was not us, it was him.
Who did you see?
Who did you ask for?

+*Remember*+ that pronouns must agree with their antecedents in number, gender, and person.

CORRECT THE FOLLOWING ERRORS.

Every boy must read their own sentences.
I gave the horse oats, but he would not eat it.
Every one must read it for themselves.
I took up the little boy, and set it on my knee.

+*Remember*+ that the relative *who* represents persons; *which*, animals and things; *that*, persons, animals, and things; and *what*, things.

CORRECT THE FOLLOWING ERRORS.

I have a dog who runs to meet me.
The boy which I met was quite lame.
Those which live in glass houses must not throw stones.

REVIEW QUESTIONS.

+To the Teacher+.—For "Schemes," see p. 186.

How many modifications have nouns and pronouns? Name and define each. How many persons are there? Define each. How many cases are there? Define each. How do you determine the case of an explanatory noun or pronoun? What is declension? How are the forms *mine, yours*, etc., now used? What is the rule for forming the possessive case? What words are used only in the nominative case? What words are used only in the objective case? [Footnote: *Her* is used in the possessive case also.] How do you determine the number, gender, and person of pronouns?

NOUNS AND PRONOUNS—PARSING.

+To the Teacher+.—For general "Scheme" for parsing, see p. 189.

Select and parse all the nouns and pronouns in Lesson 53.

+Model for Written Parsing+.—*Elizabeth's favorite, Raleigh, was beheaded by James I.*

Elizabeth's
CLASSIFICATION. *Nouns.*
       Kind. Prop.
MODIFICATIONS. *Person*. 3d
       Number. Sing.
       Gender. Fem.
       Case. Pos.
SYNTAX. Pos. Mod. of *favorite*.

favorite
CLASSIFICATION. *Nouns.*
       Kind. Com.
MODIFICATIONS. *Person*. 3d
       Number. Sing.
       Gender. Mas.

Case. Nom.
SYNTAX. Sub. of *was beheaded*.

Raleigh
CLASSIFICATION. *Nouns.*
    Kind. Prop.
MODIFICATIONS. *Person*. 3d
    Number. Sing.
    Gender. Mas.
    Case. Nom.
SYNTAX. Exp. Mod. of *favorite*.

James I.
CLASSIFICATION. *Nouns.*
    Kind. Prop.
MODIFICATIONS. *Person*. 3d
    Number. Sing.
    Gender. Mas.
    Case. Obj.
SYNTAX. Prin. word after *by*.

+To the Teacher+.—Select other exercises, and continue this work as long as it may be profitable. See Lessons 56, 57, 61, 64, and 65.

COMPARISON OF ADJECTIVES.

+Adjectives have one modification;+ viz., *Comparison*.

DEFINITIONS.

+*Comparison* is a modification of the adjective to express the relative degree of the quality in the things compared+.

+The *Positive degree* expresses the simple quality+.

+The *Comparative degree* expresses a greater or a less degree of the quality+.

+The *Superlative degree* expresses the greatest or the least degree of the quality+.

+RULE.—Adjectives are regularly compared by adding *er* to the positive to form the comparative, and *est* to the positive to form the superlative+.

Adjectives of one syllable are *generally* compared regularly; adjectives of two or more syllables are often compared by prefixing *more* and *most*.

When there are two correct forms, choose the one that can be more easily pronounced.

Compare the following adjectives. For the spelling, consult your dictionaries.

Model.—*Positive. Comparative. Superlative.*
   Lovely, lovelier, loveliest; *or*
   lovely, more lovely, most lovely.

Tame, warm, beautiful, brilliant, amiable, high, mad, greedy, pretty, hot.

Some adjectives are compared *irregularly*. Learn the following forms.

Positive. Comparative. Superlative.
Good, better, best.
Bad, |
Evil, + worse, worst.
Ill, |
Little, less, least.
Much, |
Many, | more, most.

COMPARISON OF ADJECTIVES AND ADVERBS.

+*Remember*+ that, when two things or groups of things are compared, the *comparative* degree is commonly used; when more than two, the *superlative* is employed.

+*Caution*+.—Adjectives should not be *doubly* compared.

CORRECT THE FOLLOWING ERRORS.

Of all the boys, George is the more industrious.
Peter was older than the twelve apostles.
Which is the longer of the rivers of America?
This was the most unkindest cut of all.
He chose a more humbler part.
My hat is more handsomer than yours.
The younger of those three boys is the smarter.
Which is the more northerly, Maine, Oregon, or Minnesota?

+*Caution*+.—Do not use adjectives and adverbs extravagantly.

CORRECT THE FOLLOWING ERRORS.

The weather is horrid.
That dress is perfectly awful.
Your coat sits frightfully.
We had an awfully good time.
This is a tremendously hard lesson.
Harry is a mighty nice boy.

+Remember+ that adjectives whose meaning does not admit of different degrees cannot be compared; as, *every, universal*.

Use in the three different degrees such of the following adjectives as admit of comparison.

All, serene, excellent, immortal, first, two, total, infinite, three-legged, bright.

+Adverbs+ are compared in the same manner as adjectives. The following are compared regularly. Compare them.

Fast, often, soon, late, early.

In the preceding and in the following list, find words that may be used as adjectives.

The following are compared irregularly. Learn them.

Pos. Comp. Sup.
_____ _____ _____

Badly, Ill, worse, worst.
Well, better, best.
Little, less, least.
Much, more, most.
Far, farther, farthest.

Adverbs ending in *ly* are generally compared by prefixing *more* and *most*. Compare the following.

Firmly, gracefully, actively, easily.

+To the Teacher+.—Let the pupils select and parse all the adjectives and adverbs in Lesson 27. For forms, see p. 189. Select other exercises, and continue the work as long as it is profitable. See "Schemes" for review, p. 188.

REVIEW QUESTIONS.

How is a noun parsed? What modification have adjectives? What is comparison? How many degrees of comparison are there? Define each. How are adjectives regularly compared? Distinguish the uses of the comparative and the superlative degree. Give the directions for using adjectives and adverbs (Lesson 88). Illustrate. What adjectives cannot be compared? How are adverbs compared?

CONJUGATION OF THE VERB—SIMPLE FORM.

Fill out the following forms, using the principal parts of the verb *walk*. *Pres., walk; Past, walked; Past Par., walked.*

INDICATIVE MODE.

PRESENT TENSE.

Singular. Plural. 1. I / *Pres* /, 1. We / *Pres* /, 2. You / *Pres* /, 2. You / *Pres* /, Thou / *Pres* /est, 3. He / *Pres* /s; 3. They / *Pres* /.

PAST TENSE

1. I / *Past* /, 1. We / *Past* /, 2. You / *Past* /, 2. You / *Past* /, Thou / *Past* /st, 3. He / *Past* /; 3. They / *Past* /.

FUTURE TENSE.

1. I *shall* / *Pres* /, 1. We *will* / *Pres* /, 2. You *will* / *Pres* /, 2. You *will* / *Pres* /, Thou *wil-t* / *Pres* /, 3. He *will* / *Pres* /; 3. They *will* / *Pres* /.

PRESENT PERFECT TENSE.

1. I *have* /*Past Par.*/, 1. We *have* /*Past Par.*/, 2. You *have* /*Past Par.*/, 2. You *have* /*Past Par.*/, Thou *ha-st* /*Past Par.*/, 3. He *ha-s* /*Past Par.*/; 3. They

have /Past Par./.

PAST PERFECT TENSE.

1. I *had /Past Par./*, 1. We *had /Past Par./*, 2. You *had /Past Par./*, 2. You *had /Past Par./*, Thou *had-st /Past Par./*, 3. He *had /Past Par./*; 3. They *had /Past Par./*.

FUTURE PERFECT TENSE.

1. I *shall have /Past Par./*, 1. We *will have Past Par.*, 2. You *will have /Past Par./*, 2. You *will have Past Par.*, Thou *wil-t have /Past Par./*, 3. He *will have /Past Par./*; 3. They *will have Past Par.*.

POTENTIAL MODE.

PRESENT TENSE.

1. I *may / Pres. /*, 1. We *may / Pres. /*, 2. You *may / Pres. /*, 2. You *may / Pres. /*, Thou *may-st / Pres. /*, 3. He *may / Pres. /*; 3. They *may / Pres. /*.

PAST TENSE.

1. I *might / Pres. /*, 1. We *might / Pres. /*, 2. You *might / Pres. /*, 2. You *might / Pres. /*, Thou *might-st / Pres. /*, 3. He *might / Pres. /*; 3. They *might / Pres. /*.

PRESENT PERFECT TENSE.

1. I *may have /Past Par./*, 1. We *may have /Past Par./*, 2. You *may have /Past Par./*, 2. You *may have /Past Par./*, Thou *may-st have /Past Par./*, 3. He *may have /Past Par./*; 3. They *may have /Past Par./*.

PAST PERFECT TENSE.

1. I *might have* /Past Par./, 1. We *might have* /Past Par./, 2. You *might have* /Past Par./, 2. You *might have* /Past Par./, Thou *might-st have* /Past Par./, 3. He *might have* /Past Par./; 3. They *might have* /Past Par./.

SUBJUNCTIVE MODE.

PRESENT TENSE.

Singular. Plural. 1. If I / *Pres.* /, 1. If we / *Pres.* /, 2. If you / *Pres.* /, 2. If you / *Pres.* /, If thou / *Pres.* /, 3. If he / *Pres.* /; 3. If they / *Pres.* /.

IMPERATIVE MODE.

PRESENT TENSE.

2. / *Pres.* / (you *or* thou); 2. / *Pres.* / (you).

INFINITIVES.

PRESENT TENSE.

To / *Pres.* /.

PRESENT PERFECT TENSE.

To *have* /Past Par./.

PARTICIPLES.

PRESENT. PAST. PAST PERFECT. /*Pres.*/ing. /Past Par./ Having /Past Par./

+To the Teacher+.—Let the pupils fill out these forms with other verbs. In the indicative, present, third, singular, *es* is sometimes added instead of *s*; and in the second person, old style, *st* is sometimes added instead of *est*.

CONJUGATION OF THE VERB BE.

In studying this Lesson, pay no attention to the line at the right of each verb.

INDICATIVE MODE.

PRESENT TENSE.

Singular. Plural. 1. I am ——, 1. We are ——, 2. You are —— *or* 2. You are ——, Thou art ——, 3. He is ——; 3. They are ——.

PAST TENSE.

1. I was ——, 1. We were ——, 2. You were ——, *or* 2. You were ——, Thou wast ——, 3. He was ——; 3. They were ——.

FUTURE TENSE.

1. I shall be ——, 1. We shall be ——, 2. You will be ——, *or* 2. You will be ——, Thou wilt be ——, 3. He will be ——; 3. They will be ——.

PRESENT PERFECT TENSE.

1. I have been ——, 1. We have been ——, 2. You have been —— *or* 2. You have been ——, Thou hast been ——, 3. He has been ——; 3. They

have been ———.

PAST PERFECT TENSE.

1. I had been ———, 1. We had been ———, 2. You had been ——— *or* 2. You had been ———, Thou hadst been ———, 3. He had been ———; 3. They had been ———.

FUTURE PERFECT TENSE.

1. I shall have been ———, 1. We shall have been ———, 2. You will have been ——— *or* 2. You will have been ———, Thou wilt have been ———, 3. He will has been ———; 3. They will have been ———.

POTENTIAL MODE.

PRESENT TENSE.

Singular. Plural. 1. I may be ———, 1. We may be ———, 2. You may be ——— *or* 2. You may be ———, Thou mayst be ———, 3. He may be ———; 3. They may be ———.

PAST TENSE.

1. I might be ———, 1. We might be ———, 2. You might be ——— *or* 2. You might be ———, Thou mightst be ———, 3. He might be ———; 3. They might be ———.

PRESENT PERFECT TENSE.

1. I may have been ———, 1. We may have been ———, 2. You may have been ——— *or* 2. You may have been ———, Thou mayst have been ———, 3. He may have been ———; 3. They may have been ———.

PAST PERFECT TENSE.

1. I might have been ——, 1. We might have been ——, 2. You might have been —— *or* 2. You might have been ——, Thou mightst have been ——, 3. He might have been ——; 3. They might have been ——.

SUBJUNCTIVE MODE.

PRESENT TENSE.

Singular. Plural. 1. If I be ——, 1. If we be ——, 2. If you be —— *or* 2. If you be ——, If thou be ——, 3. If he be ——; 3. If they be ——.

PAST TENSE.

1. If I were ——, 1. If we were ——, 2. If you were —— *or* 2. If you were ——, If thou wert ——, 3. If he were ——; 3. If they were ——.

IMPERATIVE MODE.

PRESENT TENSE.

2. Be (you *or* them) ——; 2. Be (you)————.

INFINITIVES.

PRESENT TENSE.
To be ——.

PRESENT PERFECT TENSE.

To have been ——.

PARTICIPLES.

PRESENT. PAST. PAST PERFECT.
Being ——. Been. Having been ——.

+To the Teacher+.—After the pupils have become thoroughly familiar with the verb *be* as a principal verb, teach them to use it as an auxiliary in making the +Progressive Form+ and the +Passive Form+.

The *progressive form* may be made by filling all the blanks with the *present participle* of some verb.

The *passive form* may be made by filling all the blanks with the *past participle* of a *transitive* verb.

Notice that, after the past participle, no blank is left.

In the progressive form, this participle is wanting; and, in the passive form, it is the same as in the simple.

AGREEMENT OF THE VERB.

+To the Teacher+.—For additional matter, see pp. 163-167.

+*Remember*+ that the verb must agree with its subject in number and person.

Give the person and number of each of the following verbs, and write sentences in which each form shall be used correctly.

Common forms.—Does, has=ha(ve)s, is, am, are, was, were.

Old forms.—Seest, sawest, hast=ha(ve)st, wilt, mayst, mightst, art, wast.

When a verb has two or more subjects connected by *and*, it must agree with them in the plural. *A similar rule applies to the agreement of the pronoun.*

CORRECT THE FOLLOWING ERRORS.

+Model+.—Poverty and obscurity *oppresses* him who thinks that *it is oppressive.*

Wrong: the verb *oppresses* should be changed to *oppress* to agree with its two subjects, connected by *and*. The pronoun *it* should be changed to *they* to agree with its two antecedents, and the verb *is* should be changed to *are* to agree with *they*.

Industry, energy, and good sense is essential to success.
Time and tide waits for no man.
The tall sunflower and the little violet is turning its face to the sun.
The mule and the horse was harnessed together.
Every green leaf and every blade of grass seem grateful.

+Model+.—The preceding sentence is wrong. The verb *seem* is plural, and it should be singular; for, when several singular subjects are preceded by *each*, every_, or *no*, they are taken separately.

Each day and each hour bring their portion of duty.
Every book and every paper were found in their place.

When a verb has two or more singular subjects connected by *or* or *nor*, it must agree with them in the singular. *A similar rule applies to the agreement of the pronoun.*

CORRECT THE FOLLOWING ERRORS.

One or the other have made a mistake in their statement.
Neither the aster nor the dahlia are cultivated for their fragrance.
Either the president or his secretary were responsible.
Neither Ann, Jane, nor Sarah are at home.

To foretell, or to express future time simply, the auxiliary *shall* is used in the first person, and *will* in the second and third; but when a speaker determines or promises, he uses *will* in the first person and *shall* in the second and third.

CORRECT THE FOLLOWING ERRORS.

I will freeze, if I do not move about.
You shall feel better soon, I think.
She shall be fifteen years old to-morrow.
I shall find it for you, if you shall bring the book to me.
You will have it, if I can get it for you.
He will have it, if he shall take the trouble to ask for it.
He will not do it, if I can prevent him.
I will drown, nobody shall help me.
I will be obliged to you, if you shall attend to it.
We will have gone by to-morrow morning.
You shall disappoint your father, if you do not return.
I do not think I will like the change.
Next Tuesday shall be your birthday.
You shall be late, if you do not hurry.

ERRORS IN THE FORM OF THE VERB.

CORRECT THE FOLLOWING ERRORS.

+Model+.—Those things *have* not *came to-day*.

Wrong, because the past *came* is here used for the past participle *come*. The present perfect tense is formed by prefixing *have* to the *past participle*.

I done all my work before breakfast.
I come in a little late yesterday.
He has went to my desk without permission.
That stupid fellow set down on my new hat.

Set is generally transitive, and *sit* is intransitive. *Lay* is transitive, and *lie* is intransitive.

He sat the chair in the corner.
Sit that plate on the table, and let it set.
I have set in this position a long time.
That child will not lay still or set still a minute.
I laid down under the tree, and enjoyed the scenery.
Lie that stick on the table, and let it lay.
Those boys were drove out of the fort three times.

I have rode through the park.
I done what I could.
He has not spoke to-day.
The leaves have fell from the trees.
This sentence is wrote badly.
He threw his pen down, and said that the point was broke.
He teached me grammar.
I seen him when he done it.
My hat was took off my head, and throwed out of the window.
The bird has flew into that tall tree.
I was chose leader.
I have began to do better. I begun this morning.
My breakfast was ate in a hurry.
Your dress sets well.
That foolish old hen is setting on a wooden egg.
He has tore it up and throwed it away.
William has took my knife, and I am afraid he has stole it.
This should be well shook.
I begun to sing, before I knowed what I was doing.
We drunk from a pure spring.
I thought you had forsook us.
His pencil is nearly wore up.
He come, and tell me all he knowed about it.

REVIEW QUESTIONS.

+To the Teacher+.—See "Scheme," p. 187.

How many modifications have verbs? Ans.—*Five; viz., voice, mode, tense, number, and person.* Define voice. How many voices are there? Define each. Illustrate. What is mode? How many modes are there? Define each. What is an infinitive? What is a participle? How many different kinds of participles are there? Define each. Illustrate. What is tense? How many tenses are there? Define each. Illustrate. What are the number and the person of a verb? Illustrate. What is conjugation? What is synopsis? What are auxiliaries? Name the auxiliaries. What are the principal parts of a verb? Why are they so called? How does a verb agree with its subject? When a verb has two or more subjects, how does it agree? Illustrate the uses of *shall* and *will*.

+To the Teacher+.—Select some of the preceding exercises, and require the pupils to write the parsing of all the verbs. See Lessons 34, 35, 48, 49, and 56.

+Model for Written Parsing—Verbs+.—*The Yankee, selling his farm, wanders away to seek new lands.*

SENTENCE-BUILDING.

Participles sometimes partake of the nature of the noun, while they retain the nature of the verb.

Build each of the following phrases into a sentence, and explain the nature of the participle.

+Model+.— ——*in building a snow fort*. They were engaged *in building a snow fort*. The participle *building*, like a noun, follows the preposition *in*, as the principal word in the phrase; and, like a verb, it takes the object complement *fort*.

—— by foretelling storms. —— by helping others. —— on approaching the house. —— in catching fish.

Use the following phrases as subjects.

Walking in the garden ——. His writing that letter ——. Breaking a promise ——.

Use each of the following phrases in a complex sentence. Let some of the dependent clauses be used as adjectives, and some, as adverbs.

—— in sledges. —— up the Hudson. —— down the Rhine. —— through the Alps. —— with snow and ice. —— into New York Bay. —— on the prairie. —— at Saratoga.

Build a short sentence containing all the parts of speech.

Expand the following simple sentence into twelve sentences.

Astronomy teaches the size, form, nature, and motions of the sun, moon,
and stars.

Contract the following awkward compound sentence into a neat simple sentence,

Hannibal passed through Gaul, and then he crossed the Alps, and then came
down into Italy, and then he defeated several Roman generals.

Change the following complex sentences to compound sentences.

When he asked me the question, I answered him courteously.
Morse, the man who invented the telegraph, was a public benefactor.
When spring comes, the birds will return.

Contract the following complex sentences into simple sentences by changing the verb in the dependent clause to a participle. Notice all the other changes.

A ship which was gliding along the horizon attracted our attention.
I saw a man who was plowing a field.
When the shower had passed, we went on our way.
I heard that he wrote that article.

That he was a foreigner was well known.
I am not sure that he did it.
Every pupil who has an interest in this work will prepare for it.

Change the following compound sentences to complex sentences.

+Model+.—Morning dawns, and the clouds disperse. When morning dawns, the clouds disperse.

Avoid swearing; it is a wicked habit.
Pearls are valuable, and they are found in oyster shells.
Dickens wrote David Copperfield, and he died in 1870.
Some animals are vertebrates, and they have a backbone.

Expand each of the following sentences as much as you can.

Indians dance. The clock struck. The world moves.

MISCELLANEOUS ERRORS.

CORRECT THE FOLLOWING ERRORS.

I have got that book at home.

+Model+.—Wrong, because *have*, alone, asserts possession. *Got*, used in the sense of *obtained*, is correct; as, *I have just got the book.*

Have you got time to help me?
There is many mistakes in my composition.

+Model+.—Wrong, because *is* should agree with its plural subject *mistakes*. The adverb *there* is often used to introduce a sentence, that the subject may follow the predicate. This often makes the sentence sound smooth, and gives variety.

There goes my mother and sister.
Here comes the soldiers.
There was many friends to greet him.
It ain't there.

+Model+.—*Ain't* is a vulgar contraction. Correction—It *is not* there.

I have made up my mind that it ain't no use.
'Tain't so bad as you think.
Two years' interest were due.
Every one of his acts were criticised.
I, Henry, and you have been chosen.

+Model+.—Wrong, for politeness requires that you should mention the one spoken to, first; the one spoken of, next; and yourself, last.

He invited you and I and Mary.
Me and Jane are going to the fair.
I only want a little piece.
He is a handsome, tall man.
Did you sleep good?
How much trouble one has, don't they?
He inquired for some tinted ladies' note-paper.
You needn't ask me nothing about it, for I haven't got no time to answer.
Him that is diligent will succeed.
He found the place sooner than me.
Who was that? It was me and him.
If I was her, I would say less.
Bring me them tongs.
Us boys have a base-ball club.
Whom did you say that it was?
Who did you speak to just now?
Who did you mean, when you said that?
Where was you when I called?
There's twenty of us going.
Circumstances alters cases.
Tell them to set still.
He laid down by the fire.

She has lain her book aside.
It takes him everlastingly.
That was an elegant old rock.

ANALYSIS AND PARSING.

1. Thou shalt not take the name of the Lord thy God in vain. 2. Strike! till the last armed foe expires! 3. You wrong me, Brutus. 4. Shall we gather strength by irresolution and inaction? 5. Why stand we here idle? 6. Give me liberty, or give me death! 7. Thy mercy, O Lord, is in the heavens, and thy faithfulness reacheth unto the clouds. 8. The clouds poured out water, the skies sent out a sound, the voice of thy thunder was in the heaven. 9. The heavens declare his righteousness, and all the people see his glory. 10. The verdant lawn, the shady grove, the variegated landscape, the boundless ocean, and the starry firmament are beautiful and magnificent objects. 11. When you grind your corn, give not the flour to the devil and the bran to God. 12. That which the fool does in the end, the wise man does at the beginning. 13. Xerxes commanded the largest army that was ever brought into the field. 14. Without oxygen, fires would cease to burn, and all animals would immediately die. 15. Liquids, when acted upon by gravity, press downward, upward, and sideways. 16. Matter exists in three states— the solid state, the liquid state, and the gaseous state. 17. The blending of the seven prismatic colors produces white light. 18. Soap-bubbles, when they are exposed to light, exhibit colored rings. 19. He who yields to temptation debases himself with a debasement from which he can never arise. 20. Young eyes that last year smiled in ours Now point the rifle's

barrel; And hands then stained with fruits and flowers Bear redder stains of quarrel.

CAPITAL LETTERS AND PUNCTUATION.

+Capital Letters+.—The first word of (1) a sentence, (2) a line of poetry, (3) a direct quotation making complete sense or a direct question introduced into a sentence, and (4) phrases or clauses separately numbered or paragraphed should begin with a capital letter. Begin with a capital letter (5) proper names and words derived from them, (6) names of things personified, and (7) most abbreviations. Write in capital letters (8) the words *I* and *O*, and (9) numbers in the Roman notation. [Footnote: Small letters are preferred where numerous references to chapters, etc., are made.]

+Examples+.—1. The judicious are always a minority.

2. Honor and shame from no condition rise; Act well your part, there all the honor lies. 3. The question is, "Can law make people honest?" 4. Paintings are useful for these reasons: 1. They please; 2. They instruct. 5. The heroic Nelson destroyed the French fleet in Aboukir Bay. 6. Next, Anger rushed, his eyes on fire. 7. The Atlantic ocean beat Mrs. Partington. 8. The use of *O* and *oh* I am now to explain. 9. Napoleon II. never came to the throne.

+Period+.—Place a period after (1) a declarative or an imperative sentence, (2) an abbreviation, and (3) a number written in the Roman notation.

For examples see 1, 7, and 9 in the sentences above.

+Interrogation Point+.—Every direct interrogative sentence or clause should be followed by an interrogation point.

+Example+.—King Agrippa, believest thou the prophets?

+Exclamation Point+.—All exclamatory expressions must be followed by the exclamation point.

+Example+.—Oh! bloodiest picture in the book of time! +*Comma*+.—Set off by the comma (1) a phrase out of its natural order or not closely connected with the word it modifies; (2) an explanatory modifier that does not restrict the modified term or combine closely with it; (3) a participle used as an adjective modifier, with the words belonging to it, unless restrictive; (4) the adjective clause, when not restrictive; (5) the adverb clause, unless it closely follows and restricts the word it modifies; (6) a word or phrase independent or nearly so; (7) a direct quotation introduced into a sentence, unless *formally* introduced; (8) a noun clause used as an attribute complement; and (9) a term connected to another by or and having the same meaning. Separate by the comma (10) connected words and phrases, unless all the conjunctions are expressed; (11) independent clauses, when short and closely connected; and (12) the parts of a compound predicate and of other phrases, when long or differently modified.

+*Examples*+.—1. In the distance, icebergs look like masses of burnished metal. 2. Alexandria, the capital of Lower Egypt, is an ill-looking city. 3. Labor, diving deep into the earth, brings up long-hidden stores of coal. 4. The sun, which is the center of our system, is millions of miles from us. 5. When beggars die, there are no comets seen. 6. Gentlemen, this, then, is your verdict. 7. God said, "Let there be light." 8. Nelson's signal was, "England expects every man to do his duty." 9. Rubbers, or overshoes, are worn to keep the feet dry. 10. The sable, the seal, and the otter furnish us rich furs. 11. His dark eye flashed, his proud breast heaved, his cheek's hue came and went. 12. Flights of birds darken the air, and tempt the traveler with the promise of abundant provisions.

+*Semicolon*+.—Independent clauses (1) when slightly connected, or (2) when themselves divided by the comma, must be separated by the semicolon. Use the semicolon (3) between serial phrases or clauses having a common dependence on something that precedes or follows; and (4) before *as, viz., to wit., namely, i. e.,* and *that is,* when they introduce examples or illustrations.

+*Examples*+.—1. The furnace blazes; the anvil rings; the busy wheels whirl round. 2. As Caesar loved me, I weep for him; as he was fortunate, I rejoice at it; as he was valiant, I honor him; but, as he was ambitious, I slew him. 3. He drew a picture of the sufferings of our Saviour; his trial before Pilate; his ascent of Calvary; his crucifixion and death. 4. Gibbon writes, "I have been sorely afflicted with gout in the hand; to wit, laziness."

+*Colon*+.—Use the colon (1) between the parts of a sentence when these parts are themselves divided by the semicolon; and (2) before a quotation or an enumeration of particulars when formally introduced.

+*Examples*+.—1. Canning's features were handsome; his eye, though deeply ensconced under his eyebrows, was full of sparkle and gayety: the features of Brougham were harsh in the extreme. 2. To Lentullus and Gellius bear this message: "Their graves are measured."

+*Dash*+.—Use the dash where there is an omission (1) of letters or figures, and (2) of such words as *as, namely,* or *that is,* introducing illustrations or equivalent expressions. Use the dash (3) where the sentence breaks off abruptly, and the same thought is resumed after a slight suspension, or another takes its place; and (4) before a word or phrase repeated at intervals for emphasis. The dash may be used (5) instead of marks of parenthesis, and may (6) follow other marks, adding to their force.

+*Examples*+.—1. In M———w, v. 3-11, you may find the "beatitudes." 2. There are two things certain in this world—taxes and death. 3. I said—I know not what. 4. I never would lay down my arms—*never*— NEVER— +NEVER+. 5. Fulton started a steamboat———he called it the Clermont—on the Hudson in 1807. 6. My dear Sir,—I write this letter for information.

+*Marks of Parenthesis*+.—Marks of parenthesis may be used to enclose what has no essential connection with the rest of the sentence.

+Example+.—The noun (Lat. *nomen*, a name) is the first part of speech.

+Apostrophe+.—Use the apostrophe (1) to mark the omission of letters, (2) in the pluralizing of letters, figures, and characters, and (3) to distinguish the possessive from other cases.

+*Examples*+.—1. Bo't of John Jones 10 lbs. of butter. 2. What word is there one-half of which is *p's*? 3. He washed the disciples' feet.

+Hyphen+.—Use the hyphen (-) (1) between the parts of compound words that have not become consolidated, and (2) between syllables when a word is divided.

+*Examples*+.—1. Work-baskets are convenient. 2. Divide *basket* thus: *bas-ket*.

+Quotation Marks+—Use quotation marks to enclose a copied word or passage. If the quotation contains a quotation, the latter is enclosed within single marks.

+*Example*+—-The sermon closed with this sentence: "God said, 'Let there be light.'"

+*Brackets*+.—Use brackets [ ] to enclose what, in quoting another's words, you insert by way of explanation or correction.

+*Example*+.—The Psalmist says, "I prevented [anticipated] the dawning of the morning."

SENTENCES AND PARAGRAPHS.

+*To the Teacher*+.—It is very profitable to exercise pupils in combining simple statements into complex and compound sentences, and in resolving complex and compound sentences into simple statements. In combining statements, it is an excellent practice for the pupil to contract, expand, transpose, and to substitute different words. They thus learn to express the same thought in a variety of ways. Any reading-book or history will furnish good material for such practice. A few examples are given below.

+*Direction*+.—Combine in as many ways as possible each of the following groups of sentences:—

+*Example*+.—This man is to be pitied. He has no friends.

1. This man has no friends, and he is to be pitied. 2. This man is to be pitied, because he has no friends. 3. Because this man has no friends, he is to be pitied. 4. This man, who has no friends, is to be pitied. 5. This man, having no friends, is to be pitied. 6. This man, without friends, is to be pitied. 7. This friendless man deserves our pity.

1. The ostrich is unable to fly. It has not wings in proportion to its body.
2. Egypt is a fertile country. It is annually inundated by the Nile.
3. The nerves are little threads, or fibers. They extend, from the brain. They spread over the whole body.

4. John Gutenberg published a book. It was the first book known to have been printed on a printing-press. He was aided by the patronage of John Paust. He published it in 1455. He published it in the city of Mentz.

5. The human body is a machine. A watch is delicately constructed. This machine is more delicately constructed. A steam-engine is complicated. This machine is more complicated. A steam-engine is wonderful. This machine is more wonderful.

You see that short statements closely related in meaning may be improved by being combined. But young writers frequently use too many *ands* and other connectives, and make their sentences too long.

Long sentences should be broken up into short ones when the relations of the parts are not clear.

As clauses may be joined to form sentences, so sentences may be united to make *paragraphs*.

A +*paragraph*+ is a sentence or a group of related sentences developing one point or one division of a general subject.

The first word of a paragraph should begin a new line, and should be written a little farther to the right than the first words of other lines.

+Direction+.—Combine the following statements into sentences and paragraphs, and make of them a complete composition:—

Water is a liquid. It is composed of oxygen and hydrogen. It covers about three-fourths of the surface of the earth. It takes the form of ice. It takes the form of snow. It takes the form of vapor. The air is constantly taking up water from rivers, lakes, oceans, and from damp ground. Cool air contains moisture. Heated air contains more moisture. Heated air becomes lighter. It rises. It becomes cool. The moisture is condensed into fine particles. Clouds are formed. They float across the sky. The little particles unite and form rain-drops. They sprinkle the dry fields. At night the grass and flowers become cool. The air is not so cool. The warm air touches the grass and flowers. It is chilled. It loses a part of its moisture. Drops of dew are formed. Water has many uses. Men and animals drink it. Trees and plants drink it. They drink it by means of their leaves and roots. Water is a great purifier. It cleanses our bodies. It washes our clothes. It washes the dust from the leaves and the flowers. Water is a great worker. It floats vessels. It turns the wheels of mills. It is converted into steam. It is harnessed to mighty engines. It does the work of thousands of men and horses.

+*To the Teacher*+.—Condensed statements of facts, taken from some book not in the hands of your pupils, may be read to them, and they may be required to expand and combine these and group them into paragraphs.

LETTER-WRITING.

In writing a letter there are six things to consider—the *Heading*, the *Introduction*, the *Body of the Letter*, the *Conclusion*, the *Folding*, and the *Superscription*.

THE HEADING.

+*Parts*+.—The Heading consists of the name of the +Place+ at which the letter is written, and the +Date+. If you write from a city, give the door-number, the name of the street, the name of the city, and the name of the state. If you are at a hotel or a school, or any other well-known institution, its name may take the place of the door-number and the name of the street. If you write from a village or other country place, give your post-office address, the name of the county, and that of the state.

The Date consists of the month, the day of the month, and the year.

+*How Written*+.—Begin the Heading about an inch and a half from the top of the page—on the first ruled line of commercial note—and a little to the left of the middle of the page. If the Heading is very short, it may stand on one line. If it occupies more than one line, the second line should begin farther to the right than the first, and the third farther to the right than the second.

The Date stands upon a line by itself if the Heading occupies two or more lines.

The door-number, the day of month, and the year are written in figures, the rest in words. Each important word begins with a capital letter, each item is set off by the comma, and the whole closes with a period.

Direction.—Study what has been said, and write the following headings according to these models:—-

1. Hull, Mass., Nov. 1, 1860.
2. 1466 Colorado Ave.,
   Rochester, N. Y.,
   Apr. 3, 1870.
3. Newburyport, Mass.,
   June 30, 1826.
4. Starkville, Herkimer Co., N. Y.,
   Dec. 19, 1871.

1. n y rondout 11 1849 oct. 2. staten island port richmond 1877 25 january. 3. brooklyn march 1871 mansion house 29. 4. executive chamber vt february montpelier 1869 27. 5. washington franklin como nov 16 1874.

6. fifth ave may new york 460 9 1863. 7. washington d c march 1847 520 pennsylvania ave 16.

THE INTRODUCTION.

+*Parts*+.—The Introduction consists of the +*Address*+—the Name, the Title, and the Place of Business or the Residence of the one addressed—and the +*Salutation*+. Titles of respect and courtesy should appear in the Address. Prefix *Mr.* (plural, *Messrs.*) to a man's name; *Master* to a boy's name; *Miss* to the name of a girl or an unmarried lady; *Mrs.* to the name of a married lady. Prefix *Dr.* to the name of a physician, or write *M.D.* after his name. Prefix *Rev.* (or *The Rev.*) to the name of a clergyman; if he is a Doctor of Divinity, prefix *Rev. Dr.*, or write *Rev.* before his name and *D.D.* after it; if you do not know his Christian name, prefix *Rev. Mr.* or *Rev. Dr.* to his surname, but never *Rev.* alone. *Esq.* is added to the name of a lawyer, and to the names of other prominent men. Avoid such combinations as the following: *Mr. John Smith, Esq., Dr. John Smith, M.D., Mr. John Smith, M.D.*, etc.

Salutations vary with the station of the one addressed, or the writer's degree of intimacy with him. Strangers may be addressed as *Sir, Rev. Sir, General, Madam, Miss Brown*, etc.; acquaintances as *Dear Sir, Dear Madam*, etc.; friends as *My dear Sir, My dear Madam, My dear Mr. Brown*, etc.; and near relatives and other dear friends as *My dear Wife, My dear Boy, Dearest Ellen*, etc.

+*How Written*+.—The Address may follow the Heading, beginning on the next line, or the next but one, and standing on the left side of the page; or it may stand in corresponding position after the Body of the Letter and the Conclusion. If the letter is written to a very intimate friend, the Address may appropriately be placed at the bottom of the letter; but in other letters, especially those on ordinary business, it should be placed at the top and as directed above. There should always be a narrow margin on the left-hand side of the page, and the Address should always begin on the marginal line. If the Address occupies more than one line, the initial words of these lines should slope to the right, as in the Heading.

Begin the Salutation on the marginal line or a little to the right of it, when the Address occupies three lines; on the marginal line or farther to the right than the second line of the Address begins, when this occupies two lines; a little to the right of the marginal lime, when the Address occupies one line; on the marginal line, when the Address stands below.

Every important word in the Address should begin with a capital letter. All the items of it should be set off by the comma, and, as it is an abbreviated sentence, it should close with a period. Every important word in the Salutation should begin with a capital letter, and the whole should be followed by a comma.

+*Direction*+.—Study what has been said, and write the following introductions according to these models:—

1. Dear Father,
    I write, etc.

2. The Rev. M. H. Buckham, D.D.,
    President of U. V. M.,
      Burlington, Vt.
My dear Sir,

3. Messrs. Clark & Brown,
    Quogue, N. Y.
Gentlemen,

  4. Messrs. Tiffany & Co.,
   2 Milk St., Boston.
 Dear Sirs,

1. david h cochran lld president of polytechnic institute brooklyn my dear sir. 2. dr John h hobart burge 64 livingston st brooklyn n y sir. 3. prof geo n boardman Chicago ill dear teacher. 4. to the president executive mansion Washington d c mr president. 5. rev t k beecher elmira n y sir. 6. messrs gilbert & sons gentlemen mass boston. 7. mr george r curtis minn rochester my friend dear. 8. to the honorable wm m evarts secretary of state Washington d c sir.

THE BODY OF THE LETTER.

+*The Beginning*+.—Begin the Body of the Letter at the end of the Salutation, and on the *same* line, if the Introduction consists of four lines—in which case the comma after the Salutation should be followed by a dash;—otherwise, on the line *below*.

+*Style*+.—Be perspicuous. Paragraph and punctuate as in other kinds of writing. Spell correctly; write legibly, neatly, and with care.

Letters of friendship should be colloquial, natural, and familiar. Whatever is interesting to you will be interesting to your friends.

Business letters should be brief, and the sentences should be short, concise, and to the point.

In *formal notes* the third person is generally used instead of the first and the second; there is no Introduction, no Conclusion, no Signature, only the name of the Place and the Date at the bottom, on the left side of the page.

THE CONCLUSION.

+*Parts*+.—The Conclusion consists of the +*Complimentary Close*+ and the +*Signature*+. The forms of the Complimentary Close are many, and are determined by the relations of the writer to the one addressed. In letters of *friendship* you may use *Your sincere friend; Yours affectionately ; Your loving son or daughter,* etc. In business letters, you may use *Yours; Yours truly; Truly yours; Yours respectfully; Very respectfully yours,* etc. In official letters use *I have the honor to be, Sir, your obedient servant; Very respectfully, your most obedient servant.*

The Signature consists of your Christian name and your surname. In addressing a stranger write your Christian name in full. A lady addressing a stranger should prefix her title—*Miss* or *Mrs.*—to her own name, enclosing it within marks of parenthesis, if she prefers.

+*How Written*+.—The Conclusion should begin near the middle of the first line below the Body of the Letter, and should slope to the right like the Heading and the Address. Begin each line of it with a capital letter, and punctuate as in other writing, following the whole with a period. The Signature should be very plain.

THE FOLDING.

The Folding is a simple matter when, as now, the envelope used is adapted in length to the width of the sheet. Take the letter as it lies before you, with its first page uppermost, turn up the bottom of it about one-third the length of the sheet, bring the top down over this, taking care that the sides are even, and press the parts together.

Taking the envelope with its back toward you, insert the letter, putting in first the edge last folded. The form of the envelope may require the letter to be folded in the middle. Other conditions may require other ways of folding.

THE SUPERSCRIPTION.

+*Parts*+.—The Superscription is what is written on the outside of the envelope. It is the same as the Address, consisting of the Name, the Title, and the full Directions of the one addressed.

+*How Written*+.—The Superscription should begin near the middle of the envelope and near the left edge— the envelope lying with its closed side toward you—and should occupy three or four lines. These lines should slope to the right as in the Heading and the Address, the spaces between the lines should be the same, and the last line should end near the lower right-hand corner. On the first line the Name and the Title should stand. If the one addressed is in a city, the door-number and name of the street should be on the second line, the name of the city on the third, and the name of the state on the fourth. If he is in the country, the name of the post-office should be on the second line, the name of the county on the third—(or by itself near the lower left-hand corner), and the name of the state on the fourth. The titles following the name should be separated from it and from each other by the comma, and every line should end with a comma, except the last, which should be followed by a period. The lines should be straight, and every part of the Superscription should be legible. Place the stamp at the upper right-hand corner.

LETTER, ORDERING MERCHANDISE.

[Cursive:
Newburgh, N. Y.
Jan. 7. 1888

Messrs. Hyde & Co., 250 Broadway. N. Y.

Gentlemen,

Please send me by Adams Express the articles mentioned in the enclosed list.

Be careful in the selection of the goods, as I desire them for a special class of customers.

When they are forwarded, please inform me by letter and enclose the invoice.

Yours truly,

Thomas Dodds.]

ANSWER, ENCLOSING INVOICE.

[Cursive: 250 Broadway, N. Y. Jan 9, 1888.

Mr. Thomas Dodds,
Newburgh, N. Y.

Dear Sir,

We have to-day sent you by Adams Express the goods ordered in your letter of the 7th inst. Enclosed you will find the invoice.

We hope that everything will reach you in good condition and will prove satisfactory in quality and in price.

Very truly yours,

Peter Hyde & Co.]

INVOICE.

Thomas Dodds,

Bought of Peter Hyde & Co.

  3 boxes Sperm Candles. 140 lbs., @33c. $46.20
7 do. Adamantine Extra Candles, 182 lbs., "26c. 47.32
120 lbs. Crushed Sugar, "12-1/2c. 15.00
60 do. Coffee do., "11-1/4c. 6.75

                $115.27

LETTER OF APPLICATION.

[Cursive: 176 Clinton St. Brooklyn, N. Y. Dec. 12, 1887

Messrs. Fisk & Hatch, 5 Nassau St., N. Y.

Gentlemen,

Learning by advertisement that a clerkship in your house is vacant, I beg leave to offer myself as a candidate for the place. I am sixteen years old, and am strong and in excellent health. I have just graduated with honor from the seventh grade of the Polytechnic Institute, Brooklyn, and I enclose testimonials of my character and standing from the President of that Institution.

If you desire a personal interview, I shall be glad to present myself at such time and place as you may name.

Very respectfully yours,

Charles Hastings.]

NOTES OF INVITATION AND ACCEPTANCE (in the third person).

Mr. and Mrs. Brooks request the pleasure of Mr. Churchill's company at a social gathering, next Tuesday evening, at 8 o'clock. 32 W. 31_st Street, Oct_. 5.

Mr. Churchill has much pleasure in accepting Mr. and Mrs. Brooks's kind invitation to a social gathering next Tuesday evening. 160 Fifth Ave., Oct. 5.

LETTER OF INTRODUCTION.

[Cursive:
Concord, N. H.
Jan. 10, 1888.

George Chapman, Esq.,
Portland, Conn.

My dear Friend,

It gives me great pleasure to introduce to you my friend, Mr. Alpheus Crane. Any attention you may be able to show him I shall esteem as a personal favor.

Sincerely yours,

Peter Cooper.]

A LETTER OF FRIENDSHIP.

[Cursive: 21 Dean St., Toledo, Ohio. Dec. 16, 1887.

My dear Mother,

I cannot tell you how I long to be at home again and in my old place. In my dreams and in my waking hours, I am often back at the old homestead;

my thoughts play truant while I pore over my books, and even while I listen to my teacher in the class-room. I would give so much to know what you are all doing—so much to feel that now and then I am in your thoughts, and that you do indeed miss me at home.

Everything here is as pleasant as it need be or can be, I suppose. I am sure I shall enjoy it all by and by, when I get over this fit of homesickness. My studies are not too hard, and my teachers are kind and faithful.

Do write me a long letter as soon as you get this and tell me everything.

Much love to each of the dear ones at home.

Your affectionate son,

Henry James.

[Footnote: In familiar (and official) letters, the Address may stand, you will remember, at the bottom.] Mrs. Alexander James, Tallmadge, Ohio.]

[Illustration of Envelope: Mrs. Alexander James, Tallmadge, Summit Co. Ohio.]

+*To the Teacher*+.—Have your pupils write complete letters and notes of all kinds. You can name the persons to whom these are to be addressed. Attend minutely to al1 the points. Letters of introduction should have the word *Introducing* (followed by the name of the one introduced) at the lower left-hand corner of the envelope. This letter should not be sealed. The receiver may seal it before handing it to the one addressed.

END

CPSIA information can be obtained
at www.ICGtesting.com
Printed in the USA
BVHW022318280623
666449BV00015B/590